HISTORICAL SKETCH

OF THE

CHATHAM ARTILLERY

DURING

The Confederate Struggle for Independence.

BY

CHARLES C. JONES, Jr.

Late Lieut. Colonel of Artillery, C. S. A.

THUS SHALL MEMORY, OFTEN IN DREAMS SUBLIME,
CATCH A GLIMPSE OF THE DAYS THAT ARE OVER:
THUS, SIGHING, LOOK THROUGH THE WAVES OF TIME
FOR THE LONG FADED GLORIES THEY COVER.......*Moore.*

ALBANY, N. Y.:
JOEL MUNSELL.
1867.

TO

MY BROTHER MEMBERS

OF

THE CHATHAM ARTILLERY,

THIS

HISTORICAL SKETCH

OF

THE SERVICES RENDERED BY THE BATTERY

DURING THE CONFEDERATE

STRUGGLE FOR INDEPENDENCE,

Is Dedicated

WITH SENTIMENTS OF SINCEREST

ESTEEM AND REGARD.

PREFACE.

The preparation of the following sketch has been a labor of love. The attachment which the writer entertains for his old company — the Chatham Artillery — an organization whose birth was well nigh coeval with the termination of the Revolution of 1776 — whose manhood has been demonstrated for eighty years — whose patriotism has never been questioned — whose liberality and high-toned friendship have been ever warmly acknowledged — whose readiness and ability to respond with alacrity, intelligence, fidelity and efficiency to every duty devolved, whether amid the sunshine of peace, or the shadows of war, have always been freely admitted — whose record is untarnished, and whose every memory is pleasant, generous and heroic — is peculiar in its character, firm and abiding; and if this brief outline of the services rendered by the Battery during the memorable Confederate struggle for independence be kindly received by my brother members, and serve to perpetuate the lively remembrance of those days of privations, exertion, and

dangers, cheerfully devoted to the maintenance of
a cause, than which none holier ever nerved the
arm of a soldier or inspired the breast of a patriot,
the object of this narrative will have been entirely
accomplished.

The loss of Confederate records, and of private
journals kept during the recent war, is severely felt
in writing a history even as partial as this. Details
soon pass from the recollection, and facts which, with
all their surroundings, we supposed at the time were
graven with the point of a diamond upon the tablets
of memory, are, after the lapse of a comparatively
short period, often recalled with difficulty and uncertainty.

Although traditions live, and the philosophy of
events survives long after the *dramatis personæ* sleep
in almost forgotten graves, specific facts, treasured up
only in the memory, soon become confused, and ere
long lose their authenticity. As so many of the
details and statistics of the Confederate war, from the
very nature of things, exist only in the personal
recollections of the brave actors in that crisis of a
nation's fate, and as each circumstance of this eventful epoch is fraught with the deepest interest, it is
incumbent upon all who can, while the images of the
past are still distinct, to contribute in a substantial
form to the records of this heroic period. Sketches
and narratives — trivial in themselves considered —
possess intrinsic importance, and form golden threads

from which the fabric of a true Confederate history may one day be woven.

In the following account I have endeavored to confine myself to a narrative of the services of the Battery. If occasionally — as in the case of the isolation, bombardment, and reduction of Fort Pulaski, or of the illustrious defenses of Fort McAllister, and of Battery Wagner — I have perhaps overstepped the limits which mark its individual history, I trust I will be pardoned; for the mind loves to dwell upon these gallant memories, and the record of the patriotism displayed, the valor exhibited, and the sufferings there endured, is sacred to the Confederate heart.

It is an interesting fact, that at various times during the continuance of the war, the Chatham Artillery furnished from its membership to the Confederate and State service more than fifty commissioned officers.

For the first time in eighty years this venerable and time honored Company, through the force of circumstances, ceases to exist as an active military organization; but the spirit of patriotism, of friendship, of generosity, of valor, and of devotion to law, order and liberty which always characterized it, still remains unchanged and unchangeable in the hearts of its surviving members; and we hope the day is not far distant, when the true men of this Battery will enjoy the privilege of reviving the good old Company within the hospitable walls of Armory Hall, and of again marching by the side of our Washington guns within the confines of the beautiful and beloved city of Oglethorpe.

NEW YORK CITY, *December*, 1866.

HISTORICAL SKETCH

OF THE

CHATHAM ARTILLERY.

———•◦•———

CHAPTER I.

THE CHATHAM ARTILLERY in the military service of the State of
Georgia — History of the occupation of Fort Pulaski.

After calm deliberation, appreciating the nature and
the consequences of the act, aware of the already
avowed purposes of the Federal government toward
a seceding state, and firmly relying upon the patriotism and devotion of a large majority of the people of
Georgia, his Excellency Joseph E. Brown, adopting a
bold and decided policy worthy the noble state with
whose interests and honor he was then specifically
charged, late in the evening of the second of January
eighteen hundred and sixty-one, issued the following
orders to Colonel Alexander R. Lawton then commanding the 1st Regiment Georgia Volunteers :

HEAD QUARTERS, GEORGIA MILITIA,
Savannah, January 2, 1861.

Colonel A. R. Lawton,
    Commanding 1st Regt. Georgia Vols., Savannah.
    Sir : In view of the fact that the government at Washington
has, as we are informed upon high authority, decided on the
policy of coercing a seceding state back into the Union, and it

2

is believed now has a movement on foot to reinforce Fort Sumter, at Charleston, and to occupy with Federal troops the Southern forts, including Fort Pulaski in this state, which, if done, would give the Federal government in any contest great advantages over the people in this state; to the end, therefore, that this stronghold which commands also the entrance into Georgia, may not be occupied by any hostile force until the convention of the state of Georgia, which is to meet on the 16th instant, has decided on the policy which Georgia will adopt in this emergency, you are ordered to take possession of Fort Pulaski as by *public* order herewith, and to hold it against all persons, to be abandoned only under orders from me, or under compulsion by an overpowering hostile force.

Immediately upon occupying the fort you will take measures to put it in a thorough state of defense as far as its means and ours will permit; and for this purpose you will advise with Captain Claghorn, Chatham Artillery, who has been charged with all matters relating to ordnance and ordnance stores, and their supply.

You will further arrange with Captain Claghorn a series of day and night signals for communicating with the city of Savannah, for the purpose of calling for reinforcements, or for other necessary purposes. And you will arrange with Mr. John Cunningham, military purveyor for the time being, for the employment of one or more steam-boats, or other means of transportation by land or by water that may be necessary, and for other supplies (except for ordnance stores, for which you will call upon Capt. Claghorn) as may be required.

If circumstances should require it, the telegraph will be placed under surveillance.

I think from our conversations you fully understand my views, and, relying upon your patriotism, energy and sound discretion in the execution of this important and delicate trust,

I am, sir, very respectfully,

Your obedient servant,

JOSEPH E. BROWN.

Governor and Commander in Chief.

HEAD QUARTERS, GEORGIA MILITIA,
Savannah, January 2, 1861.

Colonel A. R. Lawton,
Commanding 1st Regt. Georgia Vols., Savannah.

Sir : The governor and commander in chief directs you to detail one hundred and twenty-five men, or more if necessary, from your command, with the suitable number of officers, including one or more medical officers, to occupy immediately, until further orders, Fort Pulaski at the mouth of the Savannah river.

Arrangements for the comfort and subsistence of the command have been made, and you will cause one of the military officers to be detailed to act as quarter master and commissary to take charge of the public stores, and issue and account for them under the regulations that will be furnished to him.

Additional supplies of any kind that may become necessary from time to time, will be obtained by requisition made by the quarter master and commissary, countersigned by the commanding officer, upon Mr. John Cunningham of Savannah who has been appointed military purveyor.

Each man should carry with him a knapsack or valise containing a change of clothing, 1 iron spoon, 1 knife, 1 fork, 1 tin cup, 1 clothes-brush, 1 shoe-brush, box of blacking, comb and brush.

It is desirable that a portion of your men should be relieved in such numbers and at such times as you may determine, to be replaced by new drafts of equal strength ; care being taken that the relief be made at the fort, and that it does not exceed at any time one-half the command, that the greatest number on duty may be of those somewhat experienced in military duty.

In conclusion, the commander in chief relies upon your military skill and knowledge for the discreet exercise of the service involved in this order, for the maintenance of discipline, and for the care and accountability of the public property now in the fort, and to be sent there.

The occupancy of the fort will be made under your personal direction, and you are desired to remain until proper order and system are established. This done to your satisfaction, you will visit and inspect the fort and command as often as practicable, at least twice a week.

By order of the commander in chief,

HENRY C. WAYNE,
Adjutant General.

The necessity for this prompt and manly action on the part of the executive, subsequent events soon demonstrated; and every act in the grand drama which followed, proved conclusively that this dignified, high-toned course had not been too early adopted on behalf of the Empire State of the South.

The important events transpiring in the harbor of the sister city of Charleston, the recent overt acts and acknowledged intentions of the Federal government, the manifest tendency of events to one grand conclusion, the clear conception of the issues involved, and the calm resolve at every cost to maintain the dignity and the sovereignty of Georgia, the necessity for immediate preparations, by every means at command, to brave the war of races, and stem the political storm which had been brewing for many years, and the unanimity of feeling upon the great questions of liberty, equality, constitutional rights, property and honor at stake, combined to awaken the deepest anxiety in the public mind, and to engender among the volunteer companies of Savannah a generous rivalry, an acknowledgment of responsibility, a perfection of organization, and a readiness for action, at once most marked and praiseworthy. For several months previous, unusual activity was observed among them. Accessions to their ranks occurred at every meeting. The closest attention was bestowed upon drill and equipment, and the consequence was, that at this most important juncture, the 1st Regiment Georgia Volunteers — always distinguished for its proficiency and the reliability of its membership — now presented the appearance and the characteristics of a body of regulars trained for the field, rather than of a volunteer organization of state militia.

The presence of the governor in Savannah, and the knowledge that the early occupation of Fort Pulaski by state forces was under serious consideration, awakened the liveliest interest. Prompt was the response of the volunteer companies detailed by their colonel for the execution of this important order. During the long and bloody months, fraught with dangers and privations, which marked the continuance of the noblest and most heroic struggle for independence ever recorded in the history of nations, Savannah has never been called upon to blush for the honor, the valor, or the patriotism of her sons. She sent them forth generously, and those who returned, came bringing their shields with them. Their blood has crimsoned the soil, and hallowed the recollections of almost every memorable battle fought in defense of the Southern Confederacy.

The order for the occupation of Fort Pulaski was issued late on the evening of the second, and early on the morning of the third of January, 1861, detachments from the Chatham Artillery, Captain Claghorn, the Savannah Volunteer Guards, Captain Screven, and the Oglethorpe Light Infantry, Captain Bartow, numbering about one hundred and twenty-five men, under the command of Colonel Lawton, embarked on board a steamer, and at twelve o'clock m. the same day took formal possession of Fort Pulaski in the name of the state of Georgia. No resistance was encountered, as the fort was then in local charge of simply an ordnance sergeant and one or two assistants.

The following is believed to be a correct roll of the officers and members of the Chatham Artillery who were ordered to Fort Pulaski on the morning of the third of January, eighteen hundred and sixty-one :

Captain. . . . . Joseph S. Claghorn.

Lieutenants. . . Julian Hartridge.
William M. Davidson.

Sergeants. . . . Thomas A. Maddox.
Thomas A. Askew.

Corporals. . . . John F. Wheaton.
B. H. Hardee.
J. F. Doe.

Lance Corporals. . J. A. Courvoisie.
J. A. Lewis.

Privates.	*Privates.*
Bailey, F. W.	Hertz, F. E.
Cannon, Chas.	Horton, H. P.
Charlton, A. H.	Johnston, J. M.
Christian, H. R.	Johnson, G. O.
Cass, M. L.	Lawton, E. P.
Dickson, W. G.	Miller, J.
Farr, J. M.	Scranton, H. H.
Finlayson, J.	Sims, F. W.
Gaudry, J. B.	Tilden, B.
Gray, P.	Treanor, M. D.
Gray, W. G.	Tuffts, M.
Guilmartin, L. J.	Whitehead, Geo. A.

The battery of the Chatham Artillery, consisting of two twelve-pounder howitzers, and four six-pounder guns, all bronze, accompanied this detachment, and was at an early moment posted at the most available points in the fort. A second steamer, transporting the baggage of the command, arrived a little later in the day.

The fact of the occupation of the fort was communicated by Col. Lawton in the following dispatch to the governor who was still in Savannah.

FORT PULASKI, January 3, 1861.

To his Excellency, J. E. Brown,

Governor, etc., etc.

Sir : I have the honor to report to you that the troops under my command reached Cockspur island in safety, and took formal possession of Fort Pulaski about 12 o'clock M. to-day without meeting with any obstacle. The second steamer, containing our baggage and supplies, has not yet arrived, and we are necessarily in very great confusion. I am forced to write this dispatch *on the head of a drum.*

On steaming down the river this morning, I ascertained with regret, that certain unauthorized persons had taken possession of the U. S. revenue cutter Dobbin, and are now exercising control over her in the waters of Georgia. However much we may applaud the sentiment which induced this act, it seems to me inconsistent with the position assumed by the commander in chief, and the authority by him conferred on me, that any such possession of property should be permitted except on proper authority first given. I have, therefore, felt it to be my duty to take possession of this vessel, and have her towed to Savannah to be subject to your directions in the, premises. Had I been disposed to remand the cutter to the U. S. officers formerly in charge of her, it would not have been possible, as I am informed that they have left the state of Georgia. I sincerely regret that such embarrassing questions are presented by unauthorized persons at this critical moment. I will be pleased to learn your decision in the premises.

Very respectfully,

Your obedient servant,

A. R. LAWTON.

The following correspondence sufficiently explains itself, and the disposition made of the cutter fully justifies the statement, that in this earliest assertion of the sovereignty of the state, the conduct of the governor and of those under his command was marked by a scrupulous regard for law, justice and propriety:

CUSTOM HOUSE, *Collector's Office, etc.*

Sir : Capt. John Screven has this moment handed me your note of this date in relation to the recapture of the revenue cutter, J. C. Dobbin, in reply to which, I beg, in the name of the Federal government, to thank you, and further, to state, that I received a letter from the Hon. Philip F. Thomas, secretary of the treasury, some fifteen days ago, requesting me to direct the captain of said cutter to sail for Baltimore as soon as convenient, and on his arrival to report the same to him (the secretary of the treasury) in writing, and await his orders; and that in obedience to said instructions, the cutter was ordered and on Saturday last prepared for sea, but was detained by unfavorable winds until last night, when she was taken possession of by parties unknown to me. Under these circumstances, I must ask the favor of you to direct those in charge to allow her to proceed to sea in compliance with instructions from this office.

I have the honor to remain,

Your obedient servant,

JOHN BOSTON, Collector.

To his Excellency Governor Joseph E. Brown, Pulaski House.

PULASKI HOUSE, January 3, 1861.

John Boston, Esq.,

Collector of the Port of Savannah.

Sir : The revenue cutter, J. C. Dobbin, which was seized by some unauthorized person or persons unknown to me, has, under the order given by me to Col. Lawton, now in command of Fort Pulaski, to protect government property against injury, been recaptured, and is now aground near Fort Pulaski.   You will please send a revenue boat and take her into custody to-night, and I will have her hauled off to-morrow morning and delivered to you at such place as you may designate.   I much regret the lawless seizure of the vessel, and beg leave to assure you that I shall from time to time give such orders as will pro-tect the. custom house and other property belonging to the Federal government till the action of this state is determined by the convention of her people.

Very respectfully, etc.,

JOSEPH E. BROWN.

PULASKI HOUSE, January 3, 1861.

John Boston, Collector, etc.

Sir : Your note in reply to my communication of this eve-ning is received, and I have ordered the delivery of the J. C. Dobbin to her captain, with permission to proceed to sea, as you have requested.

Very respectfully, etc.,

JOSEPH E. BROWN.

The Washington guns — two six-pounder bronze field pieces — the pride and boast of this ancient and honorable Artillery company whose birth-day was well nigh coeval with that of the United States of America — the child of the revolution, whose first captain gave an arm to his country during the siege of Savannah, and many of whose early members had testified their devotion to the cause of liberty upon more than one of the memorable battle fields of the seven years' struggle for independence — these guns, themselves the trophies of that well fought contest, and the personal gift of the commander in chief, the immortal Washington — were not brought into active service.   The repeated discharges to which they had

3

been subjected in a former century, physically disabled
and rendered them unfit for field use in the present.
Although their brave voices would have been lifted
as willingly in defiance of wrong and oppression then,
as in former days, having done well their part, their
task was over, and they were tenderly consigned to a
safe and fitting repose, whence, at the proper time,
they will be brought forth, a pledge of the existence
of this time honored company, a bond of union in
coming years, a guaranty that the spirit of both revo-
lutions lives unquenched, and that although might
has triumphed for the nonce, and the sword rendered
its arbitrament in favor of superior numbers and the
doctrines which they advocated, the eternal principles
of truth and justice still survive.

The service of the Chatham Artillery was thus
coeval with the first military act of Georgia in asserting her state sovereignty, and antedates the inception
of the Confederate struggle for independence properly
so called; although, in fact, each individual act performed in the respective Southern states looking
towards their separation from a union which had long
before ceased to be equal in its benefits or desirable
in its influences, constituted but an essential, component part of that great and heroic undertaking.   From
the morning when its first detachment — buoyant with
patriotic hope, and fired with high resolves — crossed
the drawbridge of Fort Pulaski, to that sad day which
witnessed in the surrender of the Confederate army
under Gen. Joseph E. Johnston the virtual abandonment of the protracted, costly, and gigantic effort for
liberty, this Battery was continuously in the field, at
all times and in all places responding to every duty
devolved upon it with a degree of intelligence, with
an alacrity, and with an efficiency which attracted

alike the notice and the commendation of its commanding officers.

So earnestly enlisted were the sympathies of the citizens and the citizen soldiery of Savannah in behalf of the dignity of Georgia, so eager were they to secure every advantage which looked to her protection, so alive to the true designs of the Federal government, and so fearful that any delay might prejudice the interests of the state they loved so well, that a plan was set on foot to seize Fort Pulaski, and hold it against the United States without the sanction of the constituted authorities. This act was not conceived in a spirit of lawlessness, but was canvassed as a measure conducive to the early protection of the sea board, and the security of the commercial metropolis of Georgia, and calculated to give assurance and confidence to those, who, convinced of the necessity of asserting a positive independence of Federal rule, hesitated to indulge in any overt act declarative of the resumption of her delegated rights and the assertion of her sovereignty by the state of Georgia. Wiser counsels prevailed, however, and the contemplated movement was suspended for a few days to await the action of the governor, who was requested by telegraph to come to Savannah at the earliest convenient moment, observe the state of feeling, and, in view of the dangers to be apprehended, act in behalf of the state in advance of the deliberations of the convention of the people soon to assemble. Governor Brown, accordingly, repaired at once to the city. A conference was held, and after the step had been maturely considered, orders were issued for the occupation of the fort.

During the progress of the conference at the Pulaski House on the evening of the 2d of January, 1861, intelligence was received from a reliable source at Washington, announcing that the policy of coercion had been adopted, and rendering quick action highly necessary. Accordingly, the following day the fort was, in obedience to the governor's directions, taken formal possession of, in the name of the state, and by her regularly constituted volunteer militia.

The flag of Georgia was with due formality raised above the battlements of Fort Pulaski, and saluted. There it continued to wave in pride and beauty, guarded, honored, and beloved by the sons of Georgia, until it gracefully yielded its place to the national flag of the Confederate states, within whose ampler folds were garnered the hopes, not only of the Empire State of the South, but also of her valiant sisters who, with common hopes and kindred interests, had together solemnly resolved to imperil all in sacred defense of life, liberty, inalienable right, property and honor.

The right of any people upon adequate cause to change a form of government, the right of states homogeneous in interests, feelings, institutions and destiny, to withdraw from a union into which they had originally entered voluntarily for purposes of mutual benefit, protection and equality, whenever that union ceased to subserve the purposes for which it was designed, and no longer conduced to the general welfare, was believed by Georgia to be absolute and incontrovertible; and, although the sword has physically settled the question against her, its award cannot alter the rectitude of her position, or negative a principle which partakes of the essence of liberty, and has its home in the very heart of truth.

On the 18th of January, 1861, it was unanimously resolved by the convention of the people of Georgia in Milledgeville assembled:

That this convention highly approves the energetic and patriotic conduct of Governor Brown in taking possession of Fort Pulaski by Georgia troops, and requests him to hold possession until the relations of Georgia with the Federal government be determined by this convention.[1]

The following day the ordinance to dissolve the union between the state of Georgia and other states united with her under a compact of government entitled " the Constitution of the United States of America," was adopted by the convention by a vote of 208 yeas, to 89 nays.

That ordinance whereby the state of Georgia declared her freedom, sovereignty and independence, was couched in these simple, dignified and comprehensive terms :

We, the people of the state of Georgia in convention assembled, do declare and ordain, and it is hereby declared and ordained ;

That the ordinance adopted by the people of the state of Georgia in convention on the second day of January, in the year of our Lord seventeen hundred and eighty-eight, whereby the constitution of the United States of America was assented to, ratified and adopted ; and also all acts and parts of acts of the general assembly of this state, ratifying and adopting amendments of the said constitution, are hereby repealed, rescinded and abrogated.

We do further declare and ordain that the union now subsisting between the state of Georgia and other states, under the name of the " United States of America," is hereby dissolved, and that the state of Georgia is in the full possession and exercise of all those rights of sovereignty which belong and appertain to a free and independent state.

---

[1] See Journal p. 26.

There is no question of the fact that the occupation of
Fort Pulaski in this deliberate, manly, dignified manner, and in obedience to the express command of the
state executive, exercised a potent influence, not only
within the limits of Georgia, but also among her sister
southern states. It demonstrated to friend and foe
alike, that the work was begun in earnest and in the
true way; that there were cool heads to conceive, and
brave hearts to execute. The state was thus, prior
to the assembling of her convention, committed to the
doctrine of secession.

Fort Pulaski is situated on Cockspur island, in
latitude thirty-two degrees two minutes north and
longitude three degrees fifty-one minutes west from
Washington, at the head of Tybee roads, commanding
both channels of the Savannah river. The position is
a very strong one. The recent improvements in
artillery and the introduction of heavy rifle guns of
extended range and great power have, however,
diminished its importance as an isolated work, and
have clearly demonstrated the fact that in its present
condition it can at any time be reduced by land batteries suitably armed, and located on Tybee island.

The proper fortification or occupation of that island
will hereafter be regarded as necessary to the existence of this fortification.

Cockspur is a marsh island about one mile long and
half a mile wide.

Fort Pulaski is a brick work of five sides or faces,
including the gorge; casemated on all sides, with
walls seven and a half feet thick, rising twenty-five
feet above high water; mounting one tier of guns
in embrasures, and one *en barbette*. The gorge is
covered by an earthen work (demilune) of bold relief.
The main work and demilune are both surrounded

and divided by a wet ditch. Around the main work the ditch is forty-eight feet wide; around the demi-lune, thirty-two feet. The communication with the exterior is through the gorge into the demilune over a drawbridge, and then through one face of the demi-lune over the demilune ditch by another drawbridge. The scarp of the demilune and the entire counter-scarp of the main work and demilune are revetted with good brick masonry. A full armament for the work would be one hundred and forty guns.[1]

At the time of its occupation under the orders of Governor Brown, its armament consisted of only twenty thirty-two-pounder guns, the carriages of which were, in most instances, in bad condition and unserviceable. Dry rot had sadly invaded them. In the magazines were only a few hundred pounds of powder, and that of a very inferior quality. Such cartridge bags as could be found, were moth-eaten and valueless. Of solid shot there was but a limited supply, and there was not a shell ready for action. Implements were scarce. Not a single gun was mounted *en barbette*. The quarters were destitute of furniture. Every thing was out of order. Of ordnance, quarter master, and commissary stores, there was no accumulation. The honor and the safety of Georgia were, however, at stake, the spirit of the men was admirable, and every one with alacrity and untiring zeal entered upon the great work of placing the fort in as perfect a state of defense as the limited means at command would justify. The pri-vate ordnance stores of the Chatham Artillery had been freely contributed, and in the field guns of that company, and the small arms of the garrison, chiefly

---

[1] See Brig. Gen. Gillmore's report.

rested the earliest hopes of any ability to resist an effort on the part of the United States to repossess themselves of this important work.

To the detachment of the Chatham Artillery were assigned, as quarters, the casemates on the left of the fort, where its members could at all times be near the heavy guns bearing upon the north channel of the Savannah river. The duties of the garrison were heavy and continuous, and immediately upon its arrival all the rules applicable to military service in the face of the enemy were announced in full force.

At daylight, reveille and roll call, the morning gun, then police duty, guard mounting at half-past eight, customary inspections, during the day the men busily engaged in drilling, transporting supplies, placing ammunition, putting the guns in working order, making and filling cartridge bags, reaming out and setting fuze plugs, and generally in doing every thing which would conduce to the efficiency of the fort, mechanics at work repairing gun carriages, etc., the evening gun, and then the welcome tattoo. Sentinels were kept regularly posted, and the entire routine of guard duty was rigidly enforced. Every effort was made by the Governor, at the earliest practicable moment, to supply existing deficiencies. The old powder on hand in the magazines was consumed by the Chatham Artillery in firing the morning and evening guns; and, so soon as the accumulating supply of powder warranted the expenditure, practice was had at stated periods; all the men being carefully instructed in pointing and ranging. A commendable skill in the use of the thirty-two-pounder guns was soon acquired.

The members of the Chatham Artillery, already familiar with light artillery drill, rapidly acquired the heavy artillery drill, and materially aided in the general instruction of the garrison in this particular. The Manual of the Piece with the field guns became, during leisure hours, a favorite amusement with the infantry companies on duty at the fort.

The Chatham Artillery quarters were at all times remarkable for their neatness and good order. The *cuisine* of the company was perfect. The strictures of the blockade and the evils of a depreciated currency were then unknown. The country abounded in plenty, and supplied every comfort and luxury. The rations furnished by the state — although ample and even liberal — were scarcely touched by the men, who preferred daintier things procured at their own expense, and lavishly sent by friends. The well fed Artilleryman, enjoying his champagne punch within the comfortable casemates, little thought of the coming day when even a glass of Confederate whisky could not be obtained amid the heavy dews of Florida, the miasmatic influences of James island, or the laborious marches and privations of the campaign in the Carolinas. The mess-room of the Chatham Artillery was then at all times the abode of good cheer, and the home of hospitality. Garrison and visitors alike bore willing testimony to this — the colonel commanding post, and the governor of the state included. None worked harder or more cheerfully while on duty, no one was more punctual in the performance of the allotted task — none more jovial when the drill was over — no soldier lived better than the Chatham Artilleryman.

This was the gala day of service. The detachments constituting the garrison were regularly relieved at intervals of generally ten days, by new details from the 1st Volunteer Regiment of Georgia — a detach-

ment from the Chatham Artillery at all times, however, constituting a portion of the garrison. Thus each
citizen soldier was required to perform his quantum
of military service, and had still the opportunity of
attending to his professional and domestic affairs.
The pressure of actual war was not then upon the
land, although the shadows of the gathering storm
were daily growing larger and blacker.

It was a novel and interesting sight to observe men
of position and of wealth, of ease and of leisure,
willingly abandoning the allurements of home, and,
filled with the patriotic resolve cheerfully to do every
thing which might conduce to the general welfare in
this the trying period of a young nation's primal
agony, in coarse flannel shirts, with arms black and
greasy to the shoulder, trundling wheel barrows,
cleaning cannon, distributing ammunition, mounting,
dismounting, and shifting guns, toiling for long consecutive hours in the performance of laborious duties —
at other times, in neat uniform, with zeal and alacrity
acquiring the drill — and again, with equal cheerfulness
performing guard duty upon the ramparts, whether
the moon beamed brightly upon the placid tide, or the
bleak northeast wind came howling with drenching
showers from the cold Atlantic.

After the lapse of four years of privations, and
struggles, and battles, and wounds, and exposures, and
dangers, than which the history of wars the most
gigantic in their proportions and the most hazardous
in their enterprises furnishes none more remarkable,
we may look back with a smile upon these early days
of martial toil and training; but the remembrance of
them is manly with patriotic ardor, and redolent of
that devotion to country which has in all ages been
ranked second only to obedience to God.

A large force of negroes, whose labor was freely contributed by their owners, was, at the earliest practicable moment, busily employed in cleaning out the moat and ditches of the fort (which had been to a very considerable depth filled by deposits from the tide), and in other heavy and necessary work upon Cockspur island.

While a detachment of the Artillery was thus constantly on duty at Pulaski, the members of the company in the city of Savannah were engaged, at stated hours, in the gun-room at Armory Hall, in making fuzes and in the preparation of such ordnance stores as were required not only by the field guns, but also, as far as practicable, for general use at the fort. It is a matter worthy of record, that for several months after the occupation of Pulaski, a large proportion of the fuzes issued to that fort, was manufactured by the Chatham Artillery; and it is an interesting fact, so carefully were they prepared, that they compared favorably with those obtained at later periods from the best Confederate arsenals.

Being the only thoroughly equipped artillery company at that time within the limits of Georgia, and there having existed for nearly three-quarters of a century a peculiar pride of organization which induced both officers and men in time of peace to familiarize themselves with at least the most important details connected with the drill and general economy of the Battery, and simple ordnance duties, it came to pass that at the inception of our revolution, through the exertions of this company, many valuable supplies were furnished which could not at the time be either elsewhere or immediately obtained.

To Capt. Claghorn, then commanding the company, especial credit is due for the energy, intelligence, and patriotism with which he devoted his time, attention, and means to the company, its instruction and equipment, and to the performance of other duties most valuable to the state.

The activity of the gun room and of the yard at Armory Hall, during this period, will be long remembered.

The cartridge bags for the heavy guns at the fort, and for this Field Battery, were most of them furnished at the fair hands of the daughters of Savannah, who, from the very inception of our difficulties, freely contributed their smiles, their precious words of encouragement, their sacred prayers, and their actual labors to cheer and sustain the cause of truth and independence. The record of the patriotism, the heroic sufferings, the noble acts of the women of the Confederate revolution, is the brightest and the holiest in the annals of this world's history.

In the darkest hours of that protracted struggle how sublime their influence and example! The presence of their sympathy and of their aid, the potency of their prayers and of their sacrifices, the voice of their patriotism and of their devotion, the eloquence of their tears and of their smiles, were priceless in the inspiration they brought, and more effective than an army with banners.

> " The maid who binds her warrior's sash,
>   And smiling, all her pain dissembles,
> The while beneath the drooping lash
>   One starry tear-drop hangs and trembles ;
> Though heaven alone records that tear
>   And fame shall never know her story,
> Her heart has shed a drop as dear
>   As ever dewed the field of glory.

The wife who girds her husband's sword,
   ' Mid little ones who weep and wonder,
And bravely speaks the cheering word,
   E'en though her heart be rent asunder;
Doomed nightly in her dreams to hear
   The bolts of war around him rattle,
Has shed as sacred blood as e'er
   Was poured upon the plain of battle.

The mother who conceals her grief
   While to her breast her son she presses,
Then breathes a few brave words and brief,
   Kissing the patriot brow she blesses,
With no one but her secret God
   To know the pain that weighs upon her,
Sheds holy blood as e'er that God
   Received on freedom's field of honor."

On the 18th of February Mr. Davis was inaugurated at Montgomery, Alabama, as president of the Confederacy; and on the 3d of March General Beauregard assumed the command at Charleston.

On the 7th of March the convention of Georgia, which had up to this time been holding its sessions at Milledgeville, assembled at Savannah, where communication with the country at large was more direct, and where the urgent wants and dangers of the coast could be more narrowly ascertained and provided for. Five days afterwards an invitation was extended to and accepted by the convention to visit and inspect Fort Pulaski. The record of that excursion has been preserved in the public journals of the day, and so favorably impressed were the governor and the members of the convention with the zeal, the good order, the discipline, and the proficiency of the garrison, that the following resolutions were soon after adopted by that body:

Resolved: That the volunteer soldiers from the city of Savannah have exhibited their patriotism in the prompt, patient and efficient manner in which they have discharged their duty in garrisoning Fort Pulaski, and deserve the gratitude of their fellow citizens.

Resolved: That the thanks of the people of Georgia are hereby tendered to the various officers and their respective commands, who, in the hour of anticipated danger and invasion, promptly placed themselves under the command of the governor for the purpose of protecting and defending the honor and interest of the state.

Although by ordinance passed by the convention on the 20th of March, the control of all military operations in the state having reference to, or connection with questions between this state or any of the Confederate states of America and powers foreign to them, and the arms and munitions of war acquired from the United States, as well as the use and occupancy of all forts, arsenals, navy-yards, custom-houses, and other public sites, were solemnly transferred to the government of the Confederate States of America, some time elapsed before the Confederacy practically availed itself of the provisions of this transfer; and, during the interim, the burden of garrisoning the important post at Cockspur, and of supplying its deficiencies, devolved upon the chief magistrate of Georgia, who, with singular industry and ability, endeavored by every means at his command to respond to the repeated calls made upon the manhood and the resources of the state.

The two regiments of regulars which the governor was authorized by the convention to raise, having been rapidly recruited, were in the month of April distributed at Tybee island, at Forts Pulaski and Jackson, and in Savannah, thereby to a great degree relieving the volunteer companies of Savannah, which up to this time had constituted the sole garrison of Fort Pulaski. On the 23d of March the governor had been empowered and instructed to tender these regiments to the Confederate States as a component part of the provisional army.

On the 1st of May, the Chatham Artillery celebrated, with interesting ceremonies, its seventy-fifth anniversary. An oration, commemorative of its history from its earliest organization, was pronounced by Charles C. Jones, Jr., then first lieutenant of the company. A Confederate flag was presented, on behalf of the wives and daughters of the non-commissioned officers of the company, by Lieut. Hartridge, and received on behalf of the company by Capt. Claghorn. A salute of eight guns was fired in honor of the day. The parade was the largest ever made in the history of the company. Fully impressed with the momentous issues of the present, and firmly resolved to respond cheerfully and manfully to the new and important duties which would soon devolve upon them as citizen soldiers, the active members of this Battery determined, at the earliest call, to volunteer in the service of the new born Confederacy. As the proceedings of this day have been perpetuated in substantial form, it is unnecessary now to dwell upon them. Suffice it to say that the fires kindled upon the patriotic altar then erected, burned brightly through after years of gloom, of privation, and of danger; and the beautiful flag then received — at once

the symbol of woman's devotion, and the ensign of
a nation's honor — full high advanced through the
darkest trials, proved ever a cloud by day, and a pillar
of fire by night, pointing the way to noble action and
heroic endurance.

CHAPTER II.

THE CHATHAM ARTILLERY mustered into the service of the Confederate States — Removal of the Company from Fort Pulaski to Camp Claghorn on the Isle of Hope — Its equipment as a Light Battery.

From the 1st of May until the 31st of July, 1861, comparatively little active service was rendered by the company. On the day last mentioned the Chatham Artillery was, in its own Armory yard, duly mustered into the service of the Confederate states by William S. Rockwell, Lieut. Colonel of the 1st Volunteer Regiment of Georgia, mustering officer. The company was received as a unit under its state organization, the commissioned officers presenting themselves under the commissions which they held from the governor. The following were the commissioned officers:

Joseph S. Claghorn,	Captain.
Charles C. Jones, Jr.,	senior 1st Lieutenant.
Julian Hartridge,	junior " "
William M. Davidson,	senior 2d "
Bernardino S. Sanchez,	junior " "

It is with sincere regret that I am unable to present a roll of the individual members of the company, who, on this occasion, enlisted in the service of the Confederate states. This much, however, can be stated, that one captain, four lieutenants, six sergeants, four corporals, two musicians, and thirty-one privates — aggregate, forty-eight — were then mustered into Con-

5

federate service.   The very next day the company
was put under orders and went to Fort Pulaski.   This
term of service, thus commenced, was coextensive
with the Confederate struggle for independence.   The
Chatham Artillery was mustered into Confederate
service for twelve months, with the distinct under-
standing, however, had with Brig. Gen. Lawton, then
commanding the military district, and who, in the
absence of specific instructions from the scarcely
organized war department of the Confederate states,
was endeavoring to organize forces for the defense
of the coast for the longest terms and upon the most
advantageous basis possible in the novel and unsettled
condition of affairs, that if he received any company
for a period less than the term specified, the Chatham
Artillery should, if so disposed, be entitled to the
benefit of the change, and have its term of service
reduced *pro tanto*.   No one at this time realized the
gigantic proportions which the impending war was
destined to assume, or appreciated even approxima-
tively its probable duration.   It was generally believed
that it would be a partial and a short war.   The
triumph of the Confederacy was regarded as certain,
and the object of this stipulation was to provide for
the contingency — which, it was thought, would very
likely occur — of a cessation of hostilities within a
twelve-month.   In that event, these citizen soldiers
who had laid aside many and weighty obligations at
home, not in a thoughtless spirit of wild adventure,
but in obedience to a clear conception of most sacred
duty, did not desire to find themselves in time of
peace constituting a portion of the standing army of
the Confederacy.

Upon its return to Fort Pulaski the company
entered earnestly upon the performance of garrison

duty. Blockading vessels were daily in sight. Most important events had transpired in Virginia and elsewhere. The plot was thickening on every hand. Rumors were rife of an expedition on foot to recapture the fort, whose armament was still very defective. The greatest difficulty was encountered in the effort to procure guns of suitable calibre. It was therefore all important that the battery in position, and the garrison should be kept in the best possible condition. By the middle of September the armament of the fort had been increased by the addition of one twenty-four-pounder and three eight-inch Columbiad guns in casemates, and two eight-inch, and five ten-inch Columbiads *en barbette*. Ordnance stores had been accumulated. The garrison had been well instructed in the heavy artillery drill. The light field guns of the company no longer subserved the important purposes which they answered upon the first occupation of the fort — when they were almost the only pieces available for its immediate defense. The Chatham Artillery was essentially a *light artillery company*, having in its possession a light battery consisting of two twelve-pounder howitzers and four six-pounder guns, limbers and caissons complete, and also the requisite sets of harness in fair order. For the time being its members had acted as heavy artillerists, but as such they could now be conveniently spared from the garrison of the fort, and it was highly important that there should be well organized mounted artillery for the defense of the coast. Under these circumstances the question of a change from heavy to light artillery duty was earnestly considered in the company, and zealously advocated by its officers. The great desideratum was a sufficient number of good battery horses. So limited was the supply of

quarter master funds in the hands of the Confederate
officers, and in such an imperfect condition all the
monetary arrangements of the Confederacy at this
period, that General Lawton, while anxious for the
change, did not feel authorized, in the absence of
express instructions from the war department, to issue
the necessary orders for the purchase of the requisite
number of battery animals upon the faith of the
Confederate government. Virginia was at this
moment monopolizing the energies of the newly
formed Confederacy. Nobly had that state — the
mother of statesmen, soldiers and heroes — bared her
bosom in the sacred cause. Against her were hurled
almost the accumulated energies of the United States,
and it required the concentrated manhood and sub-
stance of the country to respond to the emergency,
and stay the surging waves of oppression as they
dashed against her historic borders, and broke over
her ancient and renowned plains. It was accordingly deemed advisable to apply to the governor of
Georgia — who had already contributed so largely
of the means of the empire state of the south to the
support of the Confederacy — for authority to purchase
on the faith of the state the battery animals needed.
Lieut. C. C. Jones, Jr. who had not yet joined the
Battery — his term of service as mayor of the city of
Savannah not having expired — was requested to
proceed to Milledgeville and lay this matter before
the governor. With this object in view, he conferred
with his Excellency Joseph E. Brown, in Atlanta —
the interests of the state having called him temporarily
away from the capital — and was authorized by the
governor to contract on the faith of the state for the
purchase of eighty horses for the equipment of the
company as a light battery. Pending the purchase,

however, the Confederate government, upon the repeated request of General Lawton, agreed to assume the expense of equipping the Battery, and directed General Lawton to issue such orders and furnish such supplies as should be found necessary to place the company in the field as an efficient mounted battery. Major S. J. Smith, quarter master, was at once ordered to procure and turn over to Captain Claghorn eighty serviceable battery horses.

Upon this determination to change the character of their service, the members of the Chatham Artillery at the special instance of General Lawton, who, under the pressure of circumstances, had intermediately accepted several companies for a period less than a year, and who was therefore bound under the agreement made with the company at the time of its enlistment to reduce its term of service *pro tanto*, and in consideration of the heavy expense which would be necessarily incurred by the government in equipping the Battery, appreciating too, the important fact that the young Confederacy at that moment needed in the tented field, and was likely to require for many months to come, the strong arms and loyal hearts of all her sons who could be summoned to her defense, readily consented to waive any right which they had to a reduction of the original term of service.

The effect of this action on the part of the company, trivial as it may now appear, was most salutary. The war had already assumed gigantic proportions. Its thunders had been heard in Charleston Harbor, at Great Bethel, at Bull Run, at Manassas, at Oak Hill, and elsewhere. The entire north, full of resources and of men, had assumed a determined front. It was each day becoming more and more certain that the liberty and national independence, so dear to every

Confederate heart, could only be secured at the expense of sacrifices the most enormous, and after months, perhaps years of bloody toil and death. The first blush of the soldier's life was fading away, to be succeeded by a realization of the stern privations to be endured, and the exacting duties to be performed. Home, with all the holy joys which live nowhere else save within those hallowed precincts, must be, for the while, virtually abandoned, and chosen pursuits discontinued. Other companies were claiming the benefit of short terms of enlistment, and some were eagerly returning, at least for a season, to the freedom and the pleasures of civil life. Enlistments at this period may be said to have been, in a great degree, voluntary, and serious apprehensions were entertained for the safety of the coast on account of the limited number of troops assembled for its defense.

With unanimity most praiseworthy, and a readiness most commendable, abandoning all expectation of an early release from service, turning away from the allurements of home, realizing the obligations of country in her hour of extreme peril as far superior to all private or personal considerations, and responding cheerfully to the wish of the commanding general, the Chatham Artillery — the child of the first revolution — true to the principles, objects and aims which originally called it into being, remained a willing volunteer military organization in the service of the Confederacy. Let the recollection of this patriotic action on the part of this company, in an hour of doubt and of distraction, be perpetuated to its honor, and serve as an example worthy of imitation.

Preliminary arrangements for its removal having been accomplished, the company was transported on board the steamer Ida from Fort Pulaski to Camp

Claghorn, on the Isle of Hope, on the 28th of September, 1861. From this date commences its history as a Confederate Light Battery.

The attractions of this encampment will be long remembered by every one, whether soldier or civilian; and the pleasures there enjoyed will be forgotten only when the heart proves oblivious of those impressions which are formed by the beautiful in nature, and the true in friendship.

On the day of this change of location the morning report showed only thirty-four "aggregate present." Immediately every exertion was used to equip the Battery for the field in the shortest practicable space of time, and in the best possible manner. Horses were furnished rapidly, and were, immediately upon their arrival in camp, thoroughly trained. Suitable stables were constructed. The encampment was properly located, and everything done which could conduce to the comfort of the men and the good order of the battery. Every one was in earnest, and under the guidance, direction and instruction of Capt. Claghorn, who was unremitting in his exertions, boundless in his zeal, and careful in all his plans and regulations, the Battery was soon mounted, the horses, drivers, and cannoneers thoroughly drilled, requisite ordnance stores secured, and all things put in readiness for efficient field service. Within two months the company was recruited up to one hundred and seven, and on the 31st of December the morning report showed an "aggregate present and absent" of one hundred and twenty-one men.

No change had occurred in the armament of the company, with the exception of the addition of a steel rifle Blakely gun, throwing a conical projectile of nearly twelve pounds in weight. This assignment was made by Brig. Gen. Lawton commanding, and was intended as a special mark of the esteem in which the Battery was held by him, and as a reward of merit for the proficiency and skill which it had already attained. It was turned over to the Battery on the 24th of December, 1861, and in compliment to the gallant commodore, whose memory, so cherished by the brave and the good of many nations, is peculiarly dear to Georgians, was called the Tattnall gun. On the 17th of September the steam ship Bermuda safely ran the blockade and arrived at Savannah, bringing a most valuable cargo direct from Liverpool, consisting in part of eighteen rifle cannon, seven thousand Enfield rifles, percussion caps, ammunition, blankets, army shoes, etc., etc. On board this vessel was brought the Tattnall gun. It was an excellent field piece, and was held in especial esteem by the company. At the distance of a mile and an eighth, a target 4×6 feet was struck twice out of five shots fired from this gun.

It continued for many months in the possession of the company, and was present at the battle of Secessionville. When the armament of the Battery was changed, it passed out of the hands of the company, and becoming disabled in action, was abandoned by Wagner's German Artillery, upon the retreat from Bryan county, while retiring within the Confederate lines on the old Darien and Savannah road upon the advance of Gen. Sherman's army, just before the investment of Savannah.

The text-book used and rigidly observed in the drill and conduct of the Battery, was the *Instruction for Field Artillery* prepared by a board of United States Artillery officers, consisting of Brevet Major French, Capt. Barry and Brevet Major Hunt. Schools of instruction were regularly had. Commissioned and non-commissioned officers and men, alike betook themselves with earnest zeal to the acquisition of their respective duties, and it is not an exaggeration to say, that before the yellow jessamine had ceased to mingle its perfumes with the early spring flowers, the company was thoroughly conversant with pointing and ranging, with the manual of the piece, with the mechanical manœuvres, and with the schools of the soldier, the driver, the piece and the battery.

While in state service, and for a long time subsequent, the uniform worn consisted of the undress or fatigue uniform of the company; see section ninth of the eighth rule for the government of the Chatham Artillery, adopted at a meeting of the corps held at the Armory on the fifteenth of February, 1860. I quote from that section :

The fatigue uniform of the company shall consist of a blue cloth frock-coat, single breasted, standing collar, with a row of nine buttons in front, the coat to be perfectly plain, with six buttons (three on a side), on the skirt behind at equal distances from the waist to the bottom of the skirt; three small buttons on or at each cuff, the buttons to be gilt convex artillery buttons. The coats of the commissioned officers to be distinguished by shoulder straps, such as are used in the United States artillery service. Chevrons to be worn by commissioned and non-commissioned officers. No service bars.

The fatigue cap shall be the navy cap, blue cloth, with a wreath of gold or gilt embroidery in front, with the letters C. A. in the wreath, and the figures 1786 between the points of the wreath, and below the letters C. A.

This cap, however, proving ill adapted to active service in the field on account of the small degree of protection which it afforded, was soon exchanged for

6

a comfortable black felt hat. The rich pantaloon
with its broad scarlet stripe was also laid aside for one
of dark grey, with red cord inserted in the outer seam.
Sabres and Colt's navy revolvers were issued to the
company, and were worn for several months by all of
the men except the drivers. These, however, were
afterwards turned in, and the men instructed to rely
solely upon their guns. The commissioned officers
and sergeants of course retained their side arms.
Experience has fully demonstrated the fact, that it is
unwise to encumber cannoneers with sabres, or to
permit them to carry pistols. It is well ascertained
that the most efficient service rendered by a light
battery is when the enemy has approached within
canister range. Every moment then is worth an age,
and every discharge is big with momentous consequences. Just at this crisis, under the excitement of
the moment, and yielding to the natural impulse of
personal protection, artillerists, especially when unaccustomed to the duties growing out of hotly contested
engagements, if armed with pistols, will draw and use
them. This at once terminates the efficiency of the
battery, whose firing, in resisting a charge, should be
manfully sustained to the last degree, and even to the
very mouths of the cannon. Everything, therefore,
which calls off the attention of the men from their
guns, and tends to interrupt that sole and absolute
reliance which they should repose in their appropriate
weapons, ought to be mercilessly excluded.

It was not until these fatigue suits were fairly worn
out, that the company appeared in the uniform prescribed by the Confederate regulations. The issue
of clothing to troops in Confederate service was, from
the nature of the case, very tardy; and those first
in the field — composed as they were in great mea-

sure of the volunteer military organizations already in existence and in commission — appeared in their accustomed uniforms.

It is a matter of history in Georgia, and, if our information is correct, within the limits of all the states struggling for independence, that there was not a single company, or battalion, or regiment of the United States army, which, in an organized capacity, espoused the Confederate cause. Brave officers there were who resigned their commissions in the army and navy and bared their breasts in behalf of southern freedom. To their skill, bravery, and abilities, the Confederacy owes a debt of gratitude, which, although it can never be recognized in a national capacity, will be ardently acknowledged by the stout hearts which have swelled to noble deeds of valor under their leadership, and honorably transmitted for the recognition of true lovers of liberty and disinterested patriotism.

The entire file of the standing army of the United States was opposed in an organized capacity to the Confederacy at the very inception of this momentous contest.

The appointments of Camp Claghorn were perfect in every particular. The captain of the corps in whose honor it was called, with the liberality characteristic of him as a gentleman, placed everything at his delightful summer retreat at the disposal of his command. The consequence was, that every convenience was enjoyed for hospital purposes, for the preservation of quarter master and commissary stores, the erection of stables, kitchens, and artificers' shops, and the proper and pleasant location of the entire encampment. The snow white tents, with their neat floors and comfortable camp-cots, contrasted charmingly with the grand old oaks and beautiful cedars which threw their protecting shadows above and around.

The adjacent river proved a never failing source of amusement to the old guard. Abundant supplies of fish rewarded the easy toil of the members off duty, and the piscatorial success of Tom F., will consecrate him for all time in the history of this period, as our fisherman, *primus inter pares*. I can see him now, seated upon the outer bench of the bath-house, the soft southeast wind wooing the swelling tide, the sinking sun forgetting his noon-tide wrath, and flooding the wide-extended marshes and the low-lying islands with a subdued light, as, with the patient skill of a modern Sir Isaac, he secured the finest fish of the river. I can still note the quiet smile of satisfaction with which he exhibits to his admiring comrades the result of his afternoon's sport, and remember the expressions of sincere pleasure with which he makes them the happy sharers in the good fortune of the hour.

The stables for the battery animals, with their neat stalls well drained and newly sanded, with harness-racks and blacksmith shop hard by, were always kept in the best possible condition under the admirable management of Stable Sergeant D., familiarly known as the Old Commodore.

And who will forget the quarter master's department, or rather Quarter Master Sergeant G., a three hundred pounder, if an ounce, the very impersonation of good cheer, and at all times gay and light of heart as a genuine Frenchman fresh from the vine-clad hills of *la belle France?* We have seen him scores of times at the door of his sanctum, consecrated by the presence of sundry barrels of bacon, mess-beef, flour, grist, molasses, *et id omne genus*, coatless and vestless, the sleeves of his generous merino well rolled back, his rubicund face and most comfortable figure expressive of every good nature and every good living, as at early morning he dealt out with unerring judgment upon his cracked government scales, to *Secesh Mess*, to *Sprouts Mess*, to *Live Oak Mess*, to *Dixie Mess*, to *Jeff Davis Mess*, to *Bartow Mess*, to *Beauregard Mess*, to *Confederate Mess*, to *Rebel Mess*, to *Our Mess*, the weekly allowance of commissary stores, with sundry valuable recipes as to the best method of preparing rye-coffee so that it could not be distinguished from true Java, and many fatherly suggestions with reference to the most economical modes of using half rations of sugar, soap, candles and salt.

A few hours later, and you find him, his labors for the day all done, in front of his tent shaded by the wide-spreading cedar, emitting ceaseless volumes of smoke from his ever faithful companion, a genuine red-clay pipe with a full grown Indian titi stem, surrounded by every one off duty, telling the last joke of the season, discussing the recent war news, and then when every other topic was exhausted, giving a detailed account of how the fire occurred at the fort, and finally with a long drawn sigh, as the conversation flagged, wishing that the war was over, and all back again in Savannah.

Ready for anything except a foot race, enjoying everything except gymnastic exercises, and afraid of nothing, Old Quarter, one of the marked members of the Battery, will not soon be forgotten. Philosophers of antiquity failed to pronounce who was the happiest of men. The problem might have been solved had they spent a day at Camp Claghorn.

Old Hetterick too, with his sweet bugle! How often

at tattoo have its silvery notes, mingling in soft cadence with the gentle ripple of the swelling tide, in perfect unison with the whispers of the evening winds as they lingered amid the beautiful trees silvered all over by the rays of a full-orbed moon, filled the air with thoughts of alternate joy and sadness, love and pleasure, peace and war. Now an aria, now a ballad, now a lively waltz, now a soul-stirring march, and now strains so soft and pensive, that they seemed the voice of a young mother in her first sorrow.

Police regulations were rigidly observed, and all prescribed inspections never omitted. The camp of the Chatham Artillery was pronounced by every one a model camp, a compliment none the less deserved, whether paid by the casual visitor, the inspecting officer, the general in command, or the fair ladies who frequently, as the shadows of evening were mirroring upon the placid surface of the river the noble oaks which adorned its banks, would lend to the hour and the scene attractions which they alone can impart.

The drill ground of the company, located on the shell road leading from the Isle of Hope to Savannah, and known as Pritchard's old field, was distant from the camp some three miles.

The proficiency of the Battery in field evolutions attracted the notice, and received the commendations of many reviewing officers. General Robert E. Lee, " the noblest Roman of them all," while in command of this department, has himself in person reviewed this Battery, carefully inspected its drill, and pronounced it inferior to none in the Confederate service. Commendation from one so noble, so truthful, and so capable, should be prized among the peculiar memories of this time honored company. To have formed

at any time a portion of the command of this illustrious hero, and to have merited his approbation, is a
distinction to be treasured with pride and self-gratu-
lation.

Visitors were often present at this drill ground to
witness the evolutions of the Battery, and exchange
words of friendship and sometimes of love, with ac-
quaintances and chosen companions.

The drill of the Battery was constant. Nothing was
permitted to interrupt it either in park or in the field.
He alone can appreciate the care and labor necessary
to place a light battery properly in the field, who has
himself reduced to suitable drill and discipline one
hundred untrained horses, and half that number of
drivers who at first knew no difference between a
countermarch and a *right reverse*.

It was a distinguishing feature of this battery that
the drivers were enlisted as such, and were exclusively
charged with the care and management of the battery
animals. The cannoneers thus relieved from all
duties of this character, were the better enabled to
perfect themselves in the manual of the piece, the
mechanical manœuvres, and the various exercises constituting the drill of a field battery.

The company always manifested a choice in the
selection of its membership, and the following method
was adopted. The name of the applicant, who was
vouched for by at least two members of the company,
was brought forward at an assemblage of the corps
convened for that purpose. If he received four-fifths
of the votes cast, he was declared elected; otherwise,
he was rejected. This rule preserved the character
of the company, and acted as a safe-guard. The
consequence was, that its members were always men
of character and of reliability.

In fact, the composition of this Battery was ever of a remarkable character, and was admirably sustained throughout the entire war. On account of its old and cherished associations, associations which brought into closest sympathy with it the good and the brave of more than two generations; because of the distinguished reputation which it had ever maintained, and the confidence reposed in it as the most ancient volunteer organization in the country, it was never a difficult matter to keep its ranks recruited up to the maximum, and from the most desirable material.

For many months the following was the daily routine of duty at Camp Claghorn: drill at the manual of the piece in park, at 7 A. M., for one hour; battery drill from 9 A. M. to 1 P. M.; at 4 P. M., drill in park in the mechanical manœuvres, and sabre exercise; target practice at 5 P. M.

The principal targets were located, one on Burnt Pot island, six hundred and twelve yards distant from the park, and the other lower down the river, on the open marsh, at a remove of about a mile and an eighth from the bluff upon which the encampment was situated.

All the fuzes used were manufactured by the company. Such was the accuracy attained in shell practice, that those projectiles were exploded at pleasure at almost any designated spot within a thousand yards. The face of the first target was completely riddled by fragments of shells from the howitzers, while our six-pounder guns, true to their aim, often sent their solid shots ricochetting clear across Burnt Pot island, and the marsh beyond, until they finally impinged upon and buried themselves in the yielding soil of Skidaway island. The accuracy of fire and the extended range of the Tattnall gun have already been noticed.

The *esprit de corps* characteristic of the Chatham Artillery, the general good will and friendship existing among the members, the alacrity and the accuracy which peculiarized the discharge of all the duties devolved, the ever present desire to excel in every particular, and the general neatness, comfort and good order, united in constituting this a marked battery. Comprising in its membership men of position, of influence and of property, men of individual pride and of true patriotism, who had left the endearments of home and the profits of private occupations simply with a view to the honorable discharge of those obligations which are due by true citizen soldiers when the nearest and dearest political rights are attacked, country threatened, and national honor and national repose imperiled by a powerful and unrelenting foe — obligations, which, in all their sanctity, can be appreciated only by patriots accustomed to the air of freedom, and by brave men with hearts to feel and arms to redress the wrongs inflicted — men too of intelligence, sensibly alive to the duties of the social relations, and standing in striking contrast to the ordinary food for armies — with the memories of seventy-five eventful years upon its head, and consecrated by associations which reminded of Washington, of La Fayette, of Jackson and a host of worthies who gave to the past assurance of its greatness, and to the present ensamples worthy of all imitation, it is no wonder that this organization secured for itself a name and a respect at once peculiar and most enviable.

To the volunteer who has parted with the attractions of home and chosen calling in obedience to the voice of his country, who has sought the field not with a view to temporary support, or as a theatre for wild adventure, who is eager, not only in name, but

7

by actual deed, and that of peril, to testify his earnest
devotion to the cause he has espoused, to the support
of principles dearer than life, the tedium of camp life,
relieved by no change of scene or the excitements
of actual conflict, very soon becomes oppressive.
Nothing but a realizing sense of the fact that he is in
very deed discharging an important duty, can at all
reconcile him to his status of apparent inactivity,
especially while others, brothers in the same heroic
struggle, are elsewhere winning praises and reaping
the rewards of valor upon the field of battle.

Often did the stout hearts of the Chatham artillerymen yearn for orders which would take them from the
peaceful shades of Camp Claghorn to the post of hard-
ship and of danger. Again and again did they crave
the privilege of testifying, amid the blood and carnage
of the front, their devotion to the cause of the Confederacy, and of winning new honors for their battery.
When General Lawton was ordered to Virginia, the
company petitioned to be allowed to accompany his
brigade. Special application was made by the general to be permitted to include this efficient battery in
his command, but the response was, the Chatham
Artillery must be reserved for the present for coast
defense.

On the 30th of October the first hostile guns were
heard at the encampment of the Battery. On that
day launches from a blockading vessel attempted to
set fire to a schooner which had stranded near the
Confederate battery on the north point of Warsaw
island. The battery, at that time garrisoned by the
Republican Blues of Savannah, opened fire upon
them. The enemy replied, and for a while quite an
animated little engagement ensued, which was terminated by the withdrawal of the Federals without

accomplishing their purpose. This little affair is memorable as being the first passage of arms on the coast of Georgia.

Twelve days after, this battery was abandoned and its armament and ordnance stores were safely transferred to Skidaway island.

The original line for the defense of the sea-coast of Georgia contemplated the construction of small earth-works at every ship-channel entrance from Tybee island to Fernandina; briefly thus, a small battery on Tybee island as an outpost to Fort Pulaski, a small battery on Warsaw island as an advanced work to the Skidaway island batteries, at Ossabaw no defense exterior to the battery on Green island, then Fort McAllister near the mouth of the Great Ogeechee river, a small battery on the north point of St. Catharine's island, and so on to the south end of Cumberland island. The armament intended for these batteries consisted of from three to five guns each, chiefly thirty-two-pounders. Such outer defenses were of course far too weak to repel any formidable attack, and were mainly designed to quiet the fears of the planters on the coast, who were apprehensive of the approach of small vessels and marauding parties sent to annoy and disorganize their estates. These small outer batteries were held but a short time; their isolated positions, feeble armaments, and unfinished condition, rendering them untenable in the event of a serious demonstration. On the 18th of February, 1862, the batteries erected on St. Simons and Jekyl islands for the defense of Brunswick were abandoned, and their armaments successfully removed. Thus the coast defenses of Georgia were narrowed to the protection of Savannah, the commercial metropolis of the state.

The original line for the defense of Savannah embraced a battery at Red Bluff, thence Fort Pulaski, and, extending along Wilmington, Skidaway and Green islands, included Fort McAllister, thus protecting the entrance to the Savannah, Warsaw and Great Ogeechee rivers. There was also an inner line of water batteries commencing at Fort Jackson, and including Fort Bartow, and the works at Caustons Bluff, on Whitmarsh island, at Greenwich, Thunderbolt, Isle of Hope, Beulah and Rose-Dew. The battery on Skidaway island was abandoned in March, 1862, and its guns were retired to reinforce Thunderbolt battery. The battery on Green island was dismantled about the same time, and its armament transferred to Beulah. In addition to these a line of formidable field works, armed with siege guns, was subsequently erected for the defense of the city; the left of which rested on the Savannah river at Fort Boggs, thence extending south and west in semi-circular form and completely surrounding the city at distances varying from one to two and a quarter miles. That line terminated at the low grounds of the Springfield plantation near Laurel Grove Cemetery. Historically interesting as would be a specific account of the position, armaments and uses of these respective batteries, as well as of the western lines erected for the protection of the city against the advance of the Federal army under General Sherman, and of the batteries of the Savannah river, the object of this sketch will not permit much more than a general allusion to their existence.

On the 7th of November, 1861, the following memorandum was entered upon the guard report: 9.25 A. M., heavy cannonading heard in the direction of Port Royal, continuing incessantly until 11.15 A. M., when there appeared to be an intermission of some six minutes. 11.21 A. M., cannonading recommenced, and continued until 12.10 P. M., when another cessation of ten minutes occurred, after which it recommenced, continuing until 1.25 P. M. At 1.35 P. M., the cannonading was again heard, continuing at intervals until 2.10 P. M., when it ceased."

Well do I remember that day. The morning was clear and beautiful. A swelling tide nearly at the full was leisurely rolling in, aided by a light breeze from the northeast. The temperature was delightful, and the atmosphere unusually translucent and transmissive. The first gun which rent the still air was followed by others in rapid succession, which made the glasses and the window frames in the officers' quarters rattle. We left our seats at the breakfast table, from which we were just rising for guard mounting, and hastened to the bluff in front of the house. The shore was alive with men from the camp, attracted by the continuous reports of heavy guns as they came borne upon the waters with a distinctness which told but too plainly the terrific character of the cannonading.

We at once conjectured that we were listening to the long anticipated attack upon the Port Royal batteries. Most of us, never before having heard heavy cannonading, possessed no standard of comparison; but to our ears the present bombardment seemed, as it certainly was, most unusual and severe. The discharges could be distinctly counted, and at times three per second were accurately noted.

Never shall I forget the expressions of regret which were heard on every side that we were not present to lend a helping hand to our brothers in arms of a sister state, in this the hour of extreme

peril.   Impressed with the belief, based upon the
statements which had again and again been reiterated,
that the Confederate batteries, Forts Walker and
Beauregard were powerful, and amply able to
resist the attack of any fleet the enemy might send
against them, we confidently anticipated a successful
issue, and construed the cessation of firing into a
repulse of the Federal vessels of war.   Subsequent
events disclosed, to our extreme regret and disappointment, how erroneous had been our calculations.

This reverse was a sad one for the Confederate
cause, opening up as it did the sea-coast of South
Carolina to a very great extent, and securing to the
enemy the possession of a magnificent harbor affording every advantage for an extensive and thoroughly
protected naval depot.   It also seriously interrupted
the planting operations of the sea-coast, demoralizing
the negroes on the neighboring islands, and engendering
among the planters generally a feeling of insecurity.
It also assured to the enemy an ample theatre for
antislavery operations, offering a safe retreat for every
negro who deserted from his owner.

It also established a firm base for those future
operations which culminated in the reduction of Fort
Pulaski and Morris island.

The experience of this day demonstrated the fact
that guns in open earth-works, crowded together
within narrow limits and unprotected by traverses,
could not long withstand a heavy bombardment from
well served floating batteries at short ranges.   The
art of war, as evidenced by the construction of these
land batteries, was in its infancy.   Had such a battery
as Fort McAllister been erected upon the spot occupied by Fort Walker — which could easily have been
done — or had the guns in that work been distributed

along the shore and thoroughly protected by traverses, the probabilities are that this proud fleet would have retired from the contest shattered and discomfited. The military lesson taught by this defeat — dearly bought as it was — the history of subsequent fortifications erected for the defense of the coast, clearly demonstrates was not forgotten.

1861, November 27th.— A picket of three men from the battery was this day stationed at Montmollin's point. As the movements of the enemy on the coast increased, one section of the battery was permanently located there, and another at the north end of Skidaway long bridge. This disposition occurred upon the evacuation by our forces of Skidaway and Green islands. The Isle of Hope thus became the outer island actually garrisoned and held by Confederate troops; although Skidaway island was, for a long time after its abandonment, scouted at regular intervals. Exposed as it was to the approach of the enemy's gun boats and barges by the way of Warsaw and Green island sounds, it was necessary that the immediate passages should be carefully guarded. To our battery was this duty mainly assigned. It is a matter worthy of remembrance that the Chatham Artillery for months occupied this advanced position without infantry supports within convenient distances. The rules which are ordinarily observed in posting light batteries were, on more than one occasion, disregarded in the operations of the late war. Necessity, and the scarcity of troops devolved in many instances duties novel in their character and onerous in their execution.

So long as Skidaway and Green islands remained in the possession of Confederate troops, the protection of the Skidaway bridge continued to be a matter of prime importance, as its destruction would have entailed an almost absolute isolation of our forces, preventing the facile transmission of quarter master, ordnance and commissary stores, and interrupting the retreat in the event of a reverse.[1] Hence one section of the battery was kept constantly on duty there. It was relieved when those islands were evacuated and the bridge was partially consumed by military order.

During this period, upon almost every page of the guard report appear memoranda of firings heard in various directions along the coast. The enemy had acquired possession of Tybee island, of Warsaw, Ossabaw, St. Catharine's and other islands. His gun boats moved at will in the inlets, and daily increased in numbers. Our battery was in full hearing of their guns, and within the sound of all the Confederate batteries erected for the defense of the city of Savannah.

1861, December 23d.— The Battery this day, fully manned and ready for action, marched from Camp Claghorn to Skidaway island to assist in repelling a threatened attack from Federal war vessels in Warsaw sound, which, approaching very near our batteries, had fired upon the gun-boats of Commodore Tattnall convoying the steamer Fingal out to sea. Finding that she could not proceed on her voyage in the face of such opposition, that vessel, abandoning her enterprise, anchored under the guns of our batteries, and the next day returned to Savannah.

Nearly eighteen months afterwards this vessel

---

[1] There was one other bridge from Long island to the main extending across the marsh, but it was hastily constructed, unstable in its character, and liable to be swept away by the high tides.

which had intermediately been converted into an iron
clad called the Atlanta, armed with a battery of
four guns — two of which, seven-inch Brook rifles,
were mounted on bow and stern pivots, and the other
two six-inch rifles mounted in broadside, the seven-
inch guns being so arranged as to work either as
broadside or as bow and stern guns — with a crew consisting of some twenty-one officers and one hundred
and twenty-four men, fully furnished with all necessary stores, and under the command of Captain Webb
of the Confederate navy, steamed down the same
river, and in full view of the then abandoned batteries
on Skidaway island, gallantly engaged the Federal
iron clads Weehawken and Nahant, which were
lying in Warsaw sound awaiting her coming. When
within six hundred yards of the former she ran
aground, but was quickly backed off, and boldly
holding her course again got aground, and in this
unfortunate condition — from which the most strenuous efforts to relieve her proved fruitless — commenced
the action. Unable to bring her guns to bear with
any degree of accuracy upon the Weehawken (which
approached within very short range, and choosing her
positions opened fire with her fifteen-inch guns,) after
receiving four shots which knocked off the pilot
house, drove in a port stopper, otherwise seriously
damaged the armor and wood backing, and wounded
sixteen men — among them two out of the three pilots
on board — Captain Webb was forced to surrender.
The action lasted only about sixteen minutes. The
loss of the Atlanta was severely felt. Every effort
had been used, and every means at command employed to make her a formidable vessel, and it was
confidently hoped that a bright and useful career
awaited her. With her early and unexpected capture

8

these expectations perished, and the Confederate
navy continued in these waters to exist scarcely more
than an organization in name.

We bivouacked that night upon the island near
camp Skidaway, where the 4th Georgia battalion
was posted, and within a half mile of our batteries,
reaching our camping ground after dark, and parking
our guns in an old field surrounded by a pine thicket,
of whose shelter we were unable, however, to avail
ourselves in consequence of recent heavy rains which
rendered the ground very soft and wet. It was
pronounced the coldest night of the season, but soon
bright fires were blazing, and hot coffee and capital
jokes were freely circulating among the jovial messes
assembled around the burning logs. In the morning
the caps and hair of the men were covered with hoar-
frost, while in some instances the water in their can-
teens had frozen.

As a striking illustration of the degree of cold
which characterized this still, clear December night,
the fact will be remembered that our worthy quarter
master sergeant, who, after a hearty supper laced with
sundry cups of hot coffee, with his accustomed regard
for everything comfortable, spent the night in the
transportation wagon with two bales of eastern hay,
one on either side as chosen bedfellows, found in
the early morning that even his heavy beaver overcoat
and jolly person had failed to keep the water in his
canteen, which he had not taken off, above the freez-
ing point.

The demonstrations of the enemy the previous
afternoon induced the belief that upon the full tide of
the morning an attack would be made upon our fixed
batteries. With this anticipation we passed the night,
but the morning sun disclosed the fact that the Fede-

ral gun-boats had retired and resumed their former anchorage at the mouth of Romney marsh, and in Warsaw sound. Under these circumstances there appearing to be no probability that the enemy would either test the range of our heavy guns or attempt a landing at any other point on the island, the Chatham Artillery in obedience to orders returned to its permanent camp on the Isle of Hope. Three days afterwards the enemy's fleet again congregating in force and threatening our Skidaway batteries, the Chatham Artillery a second time marched over and was posted within supporting distance of those batteries. As on the former occasion, however, the vessels retired without engaging our batteries, and our guns returned to park without firing a shot.

The bivouac of the 23d is remarkable as the first in the history of the company during the present war.

The close of the year found the Chatham Artillery still at Camp Claghorn, delightfully posted in a beautiful, healthy location, carefully drilling each day, with seven field guns thoroughly equipped and ready for efficient field service, and with an aggregate present and absent of one hundred and twenty-five.

The year 1862 was memorable in the history of the Confederate struggle for independence. It opened with a fearful train of disasters, following in rapid succession, and involving in their consequences an immense loss of territory and of men. The north, recovering with surprising elasticity from the reverses which had befallen the Federal arms, and exhibiting resources unusual and gigantic in their character, had aroused herself for a renewal of the contest with an energy and an elaborate preparation which threatened an overthrow of the Confederacy. The activity, the concentration of armies and the accumulation of the materials of war which were observable elsewhere, were apparent also on the coast of Georgia. Additional troops were landed on Tybee and upon Warsaw islands, and the inlets were filled with vessels of war and transports. The enterprise was already inaugurated which looked to the isolation and eventual reduction of Fort Pulaski. Recent events rendered necessary a contraction of the Confederate lines, and the further concentration of our forces. Accordingly about the middle of March orders were issued for the evacuation of Skidaway and Green islands. This was accomplished, and the armaments of the respective fixed batteries erected for their defense were successfully retired in the immediate presence of the enemy, who were either ignorant of the movement or unwilling to hazard an interruption.

The Skidaway batteries were three in number, immediately connected by covered ways.

The middle battery mounted five thirty-two-pounder-guns, and one forty-two-pounder in the angle, all of them elevated six feet above the surface of the ground, and in embrasure. The parapet had a superior slope of twenty-one feet. There was a gallery or covered way in rear of the chambers, and by this means communication was had from one to the other through the magazines and bomb-proofs. The magazines and bomb-proofs were protected by twenty feet of earth. Each bomb-proof contained a well. The guns in each of the batteries were well protected by traverses. The advanced battery, nearest the sound, was armed with one forty-two-pounder and one thirty-two-pounder-gun. Both of these guns covered the approach from Warsaw sound, and also furnished an effective cross-fire to the middle battery. The third or water battery was intended specially to command

Whiting's point on Wilmington island, should the enemy land and endeavor to erect a battery there with a view to enfilading the middle battery. Its guns would also have proved of great service in case the enemy attempted the passage of the other batteries. Its armament consisted of one eight-inch Dahlgren gun and one six-inch rifle gun. At the time of their abandonment, these batteries were garrisoned by the Coast Rifles, Capt. Pritchard; the City Light Guard, Capt. Levy; and the Bartow Artillery, Capt. Bertody. On the 8th of March orders were received from Gen. Lawton to dismantle these batteries. On the 9th the labor of removing the guns and ordnance stores was commenced. By the 14th the work was completed, and every gun and implement successfully retired in flats to Thunderbolt battery. During these operations twenty-seven sail of the enemy were within sight, some of them within long range of the batteries. Every precaution was observed to conceal the movement. As each gun was dismounted a dummy was at once placed in position and carefully covered with a tarpaulin. It was not until the 25th that the enemy in all probability definitely ascertained the fact of the evacuation.

The battery on Green island consisted of an inclosed work, situated on the water's edge, at the extremity of the highland towards Ossabaw sound, and was designed to prevent the ascent of the enemy's vessels up the Vernon and Great Ogeechee rivers. It entirely commanded the former, but the channel of the latter being distant some two miles and a third was but imperfectly controlled by the best guns in the fort. This battery was designed by Captain, afterwards Major W. H. Echols of the C. S. Engineers. Its *enciente* was three rectilinear faces, the flanks terminating in circular bastions from which ran two straight lines or curtains meeting in a point in the rear. The armament consisted of one one-hundred-pounder rifle gun, one ten-inch Columbiad, two eight-inch Columbiads, one forty-two-pounder, and five thirty-two-pounder guns. Subsequently a smaller work was constructed higher up the shore, about four hundred yards from the main work, and connected with it by a covered way. This was a battery of the simplest formation with but a plain front on the river, having merlons at the flanks, and traverses between the guns. Three thirty-two-pounder guns were removed from the main work, called Fort Screven, and placed in position in the additional work. In each bastion of Fort Screven, and in each traverse of the smaller work there was a bomb-proof.

The Savannah Volunteer Guards Battalion, under command of Major Screven, garrisoned these batteries from September, 1861, to March 1st, 1862, when it was relieved by two companies of Col. Lamar's battalion, Georgia Volunteers, at that time stationed at Beulah. Simultaneously with orders for the evacuation of Skidaway island directions were given to dismantle and abandon the fortifications on Green island. This was successfully accomplished, most of the guns and ordnance stores being transferred to Beulah battery on the Vernon river. Skidaway and Green islands were abandoned in consequence of a change in the line of defense adopted by the department commander, Major General Pemberton. Experience had fully demonstrated the impracticability of holding the outer islands, as at first contemplated and attempted. It was therefore resolved to abandon all the islands and confine the lines of defense to the main land.

With the lights of subsequent events before us, it is

now evident that the general adoption of this policy at an earlier day would have materially conduced to the more efficient conduct of the Confederate cause. Without a navy, with but limited means of transportation, sadly deficient in guns of suitable calibre and range, with but a comparatively small number of troops in the field to cope with the gathering hosts of the enemy recruited at will at home and abroad, suffering from the effects of a blockade each day becoming more effectual, and without the requisite manufactories at home, it was an impolitic effort to attempt the control and defense of these outer islands and advanced lines — in themselves of secondary importance — whose abandonment would have liberated garrisons and avoided the expenditure of stores greatly needed for active and more momentous operations elsewhere.

The lack of concentration, and the failure to inaugurate offensive measures in the early portion of the war, when we were more nearly a match for the United States than at any subsequent period, placed the Confederate cause at a disadvantage from which the most heroic struggles and prolonged efforts failed to relieve it. The art of war, on the coast of Georgia as well as elsewhere, was learned only after a vast and useless expenditure of labor, treasure and valuable time.

March 25, 1862.— The enemy this day at half-past one P. M., landed a detachment from their gun-boats and set fire to our abandoned batteries on Skidaway island. Shells were fired at the picket there stationed, but without effect. A Federal flag was hoisted upon Miller's house, which, previous to the evacuation, had been used by our troops as a hospital. The reports of the guns and the explosions of the shells were dis-

tinctly heard and seen at the camp of the Chatham
Artillery, distant less than three miles " as the crow
flies." The Battery was at once put in motion for the
scene of anticipated conflict; but the arrival of a
courier announced the fact that the enemy had retired. The flag, which had been left flying from
Miller's house, was taken down and brought over
to General Mercer's head quarters, then on the Isle
of Hope, and the house burned.

1862, April 2d, 3 o'clock A. M.— A courier from
Skidaway island reported the enemy landing in
force at the abandoned batteries, and also at Adams'
point. A section of the Chatham Artillery was at
once sent forward and posted at the foot of the bridge
across Skidaway narrows, connecting Skidaway and
Long islands. The other two sections were halted at
the Long bridge connecting Long island with the
Isle of Hope. In this position, where we were prepared to dispute the passage of the enemy, we were
instructed to await further orders. A few hours
afterwards it was ascertained that the Federals
did not purpose a serious demonstration, and that
they had been engaged simply in a reconnoissance.
The Battery was thereupon returned to its park,
much to the disappointment of the men who confidently anticipated that the long desired brush with the
enemy was at hand. We record these incidents in
the history of the company at this period — trivial
although they may now be regarded, and unim-
portant in their results — to show the constant alarms
and the condition of readiness at any moment to meet
the foe.

It will be remembered that to the Chatham Artillery were now entrusted the protection of Skidaway
bridge, the defense of Montmollin's point, the duty

of moving to the relief of the Beulah and Thunder-bolt batteries, and of checking the enemy should they attempt an advance across Skidaway island.

For a long time it was believed, in the event of a demonstration against Savannah by land, that the advance would occur by the way of Skidaway island. After the abandonment of our batteries there, the enemy seemed fairly invited to the effort. The presence of the large fleet of gun-boats, steamers, and transports in Warsaw sound, and the extensive encampments upon Warsaw island tended to confirm this impression; but the sequel showed that the demonstrations in this vicinity were only feints intended to distract our attention and keep our forces at home, while hostile operations were vigorously pressed elsewhere.

CHAPTER III.

Isolation, bombardment, and reduction of Fort Pulaski.

Ten minutes past eight o'clock on the morning of
the tenth of April, 1862, the first gun was heard
which betokened the commencement of the memorable and disastrous bombardment of Fort Pulaski.
Almost a year had elapsed since the reduction of Fort
Sumter in Charleston harbor, when the flag of the
United States, which had so long floated in pride from
its ramparts, went down in smoke and ruin before
the rising glories of the stars and bars of the new
born Confederacy. A little more than five months
before, and at almost the same hour in the morning,
we had listened with anxious hearts to the terrific
cannonading which silenced our batteries at Port
Royal.

The winter was gone, and spring with genial smiles
and soft influences had given to every tree its most
attractive foliage, to every flower its sweetest perfumes, to the sky its purest tints, and to the ambient
air its gentlest impulses. Everything in nature was
arrayed in living green, and redolent of life and
beauty. Even the low-lying marshes had shaken off
the dull gray of winter, and were rejoicing in new life
and vigor imparted by the swelling tide, and the clear
sunbeams shedding their warmth and light over all.
The scene was so tranquil, so full of nature and that
serenity characteristic of her happiest hours, it was of

all things most difficult to realize that the iron wheels of the chariot of war were thundering at our gates, and the lawless passions of men conspiring against the peace of their fellows, and the harmony of nature.

Yet thus it was. From our encampment we could distinctly note the explosions of the shells, hear the reports of the guns, and frequently recognize whether they were directed at or from the fort. For the first hour the firing from the Federal batteries appeared to be slow and uncertain, their mortar shells exploding too high and at unequal distances. So soon, however, as the range had been obtained, the firing became more rapid and effective. The horizon was flecked with white clouds, apparently springing out of nothing, at first mere points in space, then gradually expanding and growing less distinct, until finally mingling with the circumambient air they floated gently away and were lost to sight. It was difficult at this remove to realize the fact that these innocent looking little white puffs, so evanescent in their character, had any connection with the death-dealing projectiles hurled with terrible effect from the iron-bound throats of hoarse Parrott guns, and hoarser Columbiads and mortars. The bombardment during the day continued without intermission, although the reports were less audible as the sun reached and lingered near the meridian.

In the afternoon some of us rode over to Skidaway island and remained until nearly sunset, watching the progress of the bombardment from the top of the traverse of the lower battery. With the aid of a field glass everything could be distinctly seen. The smoke of the guns from the batteries on either side rose in heavy white volumes, now almost hiding the fort from view, and now lining the low-lying shores of Tybee island. No signs of breaching could be perceived in the

walls of the fort looking in our direction. Everything
seemed to be in good working order, and we did not
for one moment contemplate a speedy reduction of one
of the strongest defenses on the Confederate coast. A
constant explosion of shells above and around the fort
gave token of the dangers which environed the heroic
garrison. Several war-vessels were lying in the vicinity, or leisurely moving about, but they did not appear
to be taking an active part in the engagement. Sometimes eight reports could be counted in a minute, and
the firing increased in rapidity as the declining sun
neared the western horizon.

During the night the firing continued at regular
intervals, and the flashes of the bursting mortar shells
were plainly visible from Camp Claghorn. With the
light of the morning the bombardment was renewed
with redoubled energy, continuing until two o'clock
P. M., when it ceased. This silence — ominous of
disaster and mortification to ourselves — gave birth in
our minds only to the belief that the Federals had
been compelled to discontinue their efforts to reduce
our cherished fort. Never for one moment did we
conjecture that its stout walls had yielded, or its
garrison surrendered. To the members of the Chatham Artillery Fort Pulaski was peculiarly dear. We
were of the first to occupy it, when, under the orders
of Governor Brown, it was deemed proper to take
possession of it in the name of the state of Georgia.
We had contributed months of cheerful labor in
mounting its guns, in placing its armament in proper
position, in preparing fuzes, filling shells, throwing up
traverses, in training its guns and in perfecting ourselves, and in assisting in drilling the members of
other companies composing its garrison in the manual
of the respective pieces constituting its battery. We

had spent days of toil and nights of watching within its walls. Hours of pleasure and of mirth had been enjoyed within its hospitable casemates. We had marked it growing in strength day by day, until we came to believe that it was invincible by almost any force that could be sent against it. But a few months had elapsed since we were a component part of the garrison, to whom were committed its sacred defense and the honor of our arms. No wonder then that the progress of the bombardment was observed by the Chatham Artillery with a peculiar interest. No wonder the members of this company looked forward with confidence to a successful issue. No marvel that the unexpected and early surrender of the fort affected them most sensibly. The first intelligence of that sad and disastrous fact was not credited in our camp.

At the time of the surrender of Fort Pulaski, its armament consisted of

    5 ten-inch Columbiads unchambered.
    9 eight-inch   "   "
    3 forty-two-pounder guns.
  20 thirty-two-pounder guns.
    2 twenty-four-pounder Blakely rifle guns.
    1 twenty-four-pounder iron howitzer.
    2 twelve-pounder bronze howitzers.
    2 twelve-inch iron mortars.
    3 ten-inch sea-coast mortars.
    1 six-pounder gun.
  Total, forty-eight guns of all calibres.

Of these, the following bore upon the Federal batteries on Tybee island :

In Barbette.

    5 eight-inch Columbiads.
    4 ten-inch   "

    1 twenty-four-pounder Blakely rifle gun.
    2 ten-inch sea-coast mortars.

In Casemate.

    1 eight-inch Columbiad.
    4 thirty-two-pounder guns.

In Batteries outside the Fort.

    1 ten-inch sea-coast mortar.
    2 twelve-inch sea-coast mortars.
Making a total of twenty pieces.

Of these, however, sufficient elevation to reach Tybee island could not be secured with the eight-inch Columbiad in casemate. Only a few shots were fired from it, and these falling short, the use of this gun was discontinued during the progress of the bombardment.

Opposed to the fort, and located upon Tybee island, were eleven Federal batteries, named and armed as follows:

1. Battery Stanton; 3,400 yards distant, mounting three heavy thirteen-inch mortars.

2. Battery Grant; 3,200 yards distant, mounting three heavy thirteen-inch mortars.

3. Battery Lyon; 3,100 yards distant, mounting three ten-inch Columbiads.

4. Battery Lincoln; 3,045 yards distant, mounting three eight-inch Columbiads.

5. Battery Burnside; 2,750 yards distant, mounting one thirteen-inch mortar.

6. Battery Sherman; 2,650 yards distant, mounting three thirteen-inch mortars.

7. Battery Halleck; 2,400 yards distant, mounting two thirteen-inch mortars.

8. Battery Scott; distant 1,740 yards, mounting three ten-inch and one eight-inch Columbiads.

Plate II.

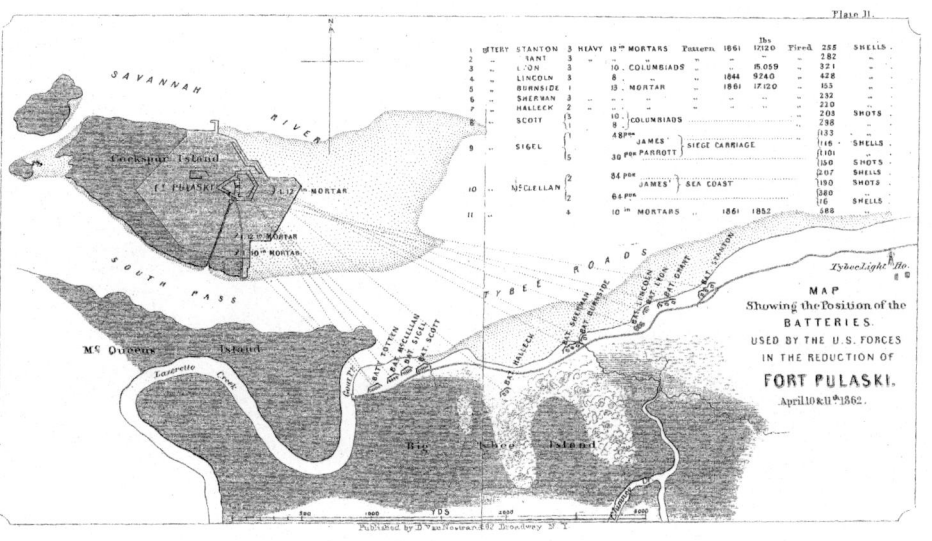

	BATTERY	STANTON	3	HEAVY	13 IN MORTARS	Pattern	1861	lbs 17120	Fired.	258	SHELLS
2	"	GRANT	3	"	"	"	"	"	"	282	"
3	"	LYON	3	"	10 " COLUMBIADS	"	"	15,059	"	321	"
4	"	LINCOLN	3	"	8 " "	"	1844	9740	"	428	"
5	"	BURNSIDE	1	"	13 " MORTAR	"	1861	17,120	"	165	"
6	"	SHERMAN	3	"	"	"	"	"	"	232	"
7	"	HALLECK	2	"	10 " MORTAR	"	"	"	"	210	"
	"	SCOTT	3	"	10 " COLUMBIADS	"	"	"	"	203	SHOTS
8	"	"	1	"	"	"	"	"	"	298	"
			1	"	48 Por	"	"	"	"	133	"
9	"	SIGEL			JAMES' } SIEGE CARRIAGE					116	SHELLS
			5	"	30 Por PARROTT	"	"	"	"	101	"
										150	SHOTS
10	"	McCLELLAN	2	"	84 Por	"	"	"	"	207	SHELLS
					JAMES' } SEA COAST					190	SHOTS
			2	"	64 Por	"	"	"	"	280	"
										16	SHELLS
11	"	"	4	"	10 IN MORTARS	"	1861	1852	"	688	"

SAVANNAH

RIVER

Cockspur Island

FT PULASKI

13 IN MORTAR

SOUTH PASS

13 IN MORTAR

10 IN MORTAR

TYBEE ROADS

Tybee Light Ho.

MAP
Showing the Position of the
BATTERIES.
USED BY THE U.S. FORCES
IN THE REDUCTION OF
FORT PULASKI.
April 10 & 11th 1862.

Mc Queens Island

Lazeretto Creek

Big Tybee Island

Published by D. Van Nostrand 192 Broadway N.Y.

9. Battery Sigel; distant 1,670 yards, mounting one forty-eight-pounder James rifle gun, and five thirty-pounder Parrott guns, on siege carriages.

10. Battery McClellan, distant 1,650 yards, mounting two eighty-four-pounder, and two sixty-four-pounder James guns.

11. Battery Totten, 1,650 yards distant, mounting four ten-inch mortars.

Making in all thirty-six pieces.

These batteries[1] were distributed along a front of 2,550 yards, and were well protected. A moment's reflection will show how unequal the conflict between the fort and these detached batteries. On the one hand the fire was distracted by a series of works, some of them well masked, all admirably protected, extending along a line of nearly a mile and a half; while on the other hand, there was an absolute concentration against a single fortification, with perpendicular walls twenty-five feet high, its entire outlines looming up in bold relief. On the one side the resources of an immense country and of the world were at command to furnish any additional supplies of men and materials of war; on the other, there was but a small garrison, a limited supply of everything, and absolute isolation. On the one hand, there were stout sand parapets — low-lying and difficult to be struck — guns carefully embrasured, and an abundance of men and materials to repair any injuries inflicted. On the other, there was the fort, whose walls of masonry were never designed to resist the momentum and the penetration of such projectiles as were hurled that day, standing solitary and alone,

---

[1] For the accompanying map showing the respective locations and lines of fire of these Federal batteries, I am indebted to the Official Report of Brig. Gen. Gillmore.

without the means of repair at command. On the Federal side there was a concentration of heavy guns and mortars far exceeding in power the batteries of the fort. Under such circumstances, and without a solitary ray of hope of relief or assistance, the fall of Fort Pulaski became a mere question of time. Its reduction was virtually accomplished when its isolation was consummated on the 22d of February.

The removal of the obstructions which had been placed by the Confederates in Wall's cut—an artificial channel connecting New and Wright rivers — afforded the gun-boats of the enemy the means of entering the Savannah river in rear of Port Pulaski, without encountering the fire of its batteries, and of covering the Federal working parties employed in the erection of investing batteries at Venus's point, and on the north end of Bird's island. Confederate batteries should have been posted for the protection of the obstructions in Wall's cut, if, after the evacuation of Tybee island any necessity existed for the further retention of Fort Pulaski. Once before in the history of Savannah, did the use by the enemy of this unguarded passage prove disastrous to the hopes of brave men contending for the possession of home, and the enjoyment of liberty.

On the evening of the 16th of September, 1779, Col. Maitland arrived at Dawfuskie island, and found the Savannah river in the possession of the French. Embarrassed, and not knowing how to effect a desired junction with Provost in Savannah (the city being at the time invested by the French forces under Count D'Estaing, and the American army under Gen. Lincoln, and a demand having been made upon the English garrison for surrender), he chanced upon some negro fishermen familiar with the creeks and marshes, who informed him of the passage through Wall's cut. The tide and the dense fog favored the execution of his plans, and he was thus enabled, availing himself of this route, unperceived by the French, to reach the city of Savannah with his troops on the ensuing afternoon. The acquisition of this formidable reenforcement, under the leadership of such a brave and experienced officer, greatly encouraged the dispirited garrison, and furnished the means of successful resistance to the combined attack which was gallantly made by the allied forces a few days afterwards.[1]

Just previous to the investment of the fort, Commodore Tattnall, with his little fleet, had, in the face of the gun-boats of the enemy, and under their fire, effected the passage of the Savannah river, and thrown into the fort a six months' supply of provisions; a characteristic episode in the life of this great and noble man, whose conspicuous valor, intrepidity, and acknowledged abilities had so long reflected honor upon the American navy, and won for it the highest consideration wherever his name and services were mentioned — whose devotion to the state which gave him birth, in the hour of her extreme peril — whose self-sacrifice, whose exalted high-toned action, whose enlarged experience, whose qualities of the head and of the heart, and whose every distinguishing trait have won for him a home in the hearts of his admiring countrymen, and a record in the history of his times which neither the lapse of years nor the fortunes of the hour can desecrate or impair. Even now Epaminondas the renowned leader of the Thebans, with his single garment, is wealthier and far more illustrious than the king of the Persians with his

---

[1] See McCall's *History of Georgia,* vol. ii, p. 255.

10

abundant gold, the tribute of unholy spoils and oppression.

The investment of Fort Pulaski was accomplished upon the erection and location of the following Federal batteries, viz : Battery Vulcan at Venus's point, mounting six guns—Battery Hamilton on the upper end of Bird's island, mounting six guns—a battery on the lower end of Long island, and a battery of three guns on Decent island, subsequently transferred to an old hulk anchored in Lazaretto creek at the confluence of Oyster creek. As has been already stated, its absolute blockade may be dated on the 22d of February. In this isolation of the fort most material assistance had been rendered by a formidable fleet of gun-boats, against whose operations no adequate resistance could be offered on the part of the Confederates.

From this period until the afternoon of the 9th of April, the forces of the enemy were busily engaged in the erection of the eleven batteries on Tybee island established against Fort Pulaski. They worked at night, in silence, carefully screening from view their labors, and at no time causing any sudden alteration in the outline of the landscape. The garrison of the fort was also actively employed in protecting the barbette guns with traverses, in securing the inner defenses of the fort, and in doing everything in their power which might conduce to the proper defense of the fortification. It was known that the enemy was erecting batteries against the fort on Tybee island, but their precise extent and location were not definitely ascertained, so carefully concealed from view were the Federal operations. Not for a moment was it believed that the walls could be breached, or the fort rendered untenable by any fire which might be

brought to bear from guns located on Tybee island.[1]
Such an achievement had never, in the history of artil-
ery, been accomplished by breaching batteries. Novel
results, however, were soon to be attained with the
aid of rifle guns, and conical shot, and percussion
shells, for the anticipation of which the military mind
had not been prepared by the accepted lessons of
former days. Three or four days previous to the
commencement of the bombardment, something like
the inception of a small battery was observed on the
lower end of the Little Marsh island immediately
above Cockspur island. A boat party consisting of
some twelve men under charge of Lieutenants Hopkins and Hussey, sent to reconnoitre, found a mortar
at this point which the enemy were about placing in
position. Unable to bring it away, the mortar was
spiked and thrown into the Savannah river by this
detachment, and the implements found with it, and
as many of the shells as could be transported in the
boats, were conveyed to Fort Pulaski. Such of the
shells as could not be removed were thrown into the
river. During the bombardment the Federals had a
mortar at this point. It was probably the same which
had been thus temporarily disabled. Its fire, intended
to take the barbette fire of the fort in reverse, proved,
however, entirely innocuous, and the shells captured
on the occasion alluded to, were expended upon the
enemy during the subsequent bombardment.

On the evening of the 9th, everything being in
readiness on the Federal side to open fire, just after
sunrise on the morning of the 10th of April, 1862,
Major General David Hunter commanding this United

---

[1] This opinion was freely expressed by Gen. Robert E. Lee, and by
other officers whose judgment and experience inspired every confidence.

States department, dispatched Lieut. J. H. Wilson of the United States Topographical Engineers in an open boat to Fort Pulaski, bearing a flag of truce, and the following summons to surrender:

HEAD QUARTERS, DEPARTMENT OF THE SOUTH,
Tybee Island, Ga., April 10, 1862.

To the Commanding Officer, Fort Pulaski.

Sir: I hereby demand of you the immediate surrender and restoration of Fort Pulaski to the authority and possession of the United States.

This demand is made with a view to avoiding, if possible, the effusion of blood which must result from the bombardment and attack now in readiness to be opened.

The number, calibre, and completeness of the batteries surrounding you, leave no doubt as to what must result in case of refusal; and as the defense, however obstinate, must eventually succumb to the assailing force at my disposal, it is hoped you will see fit to avert the useless waste of life.

This communication will be carried to you under a flag of truce by Lieut. J. H. Wilson, United States army, who is authorized to wait any period not exceeding thirty minutes from delivery, for your answer.

I have the honor to be sir,
Your most obedient servant,
DAVID HUNTER.
Major General Commanding.

To this demand, the following laconic and brave response was returned by Colonel Olmstead commanding Fort Pulaski:

HEAD QUARTERS, FORT PULASKI, April 10, 1862.

Major General David Hunter,
Commanding on Tybee island.

Sir: I have to acknowledge receipt of your communication of this date, demanding the unconditional surrender of Fort Pulaski.

In reply I can only say, that I am here to defend the Fort not to surrender it.

I have honor to be, very respectfully
Your obedient servant,
CHAS. H. OLMSTEAD,
Colonel, First Volunteer Regiment of Georgia, Com'g Post.

Upon the receipt of this reply by the Federal commander, orders were immediately issued for the commencement of the bombardment. The first shell was fired from Battery Halleck at a quarter-past eight o'clock, and soon all the Federal batteries were engaged. A few minutes after, the fort replied, and the action then became general.

As the official report of Col. Olmstead furnishes a concise history of the engagement, and should be perpetuated as a most valuable record of this memorable bombardment, it is herewith presented *in extenso:*

MILLEDGEVILLE, GEORGIA, October 1, 1862.
Captain George A. Mercer,
A. A. General, District of Georgia.

Captain: Immediately after the fall of Fort Pulaski, and while a prisoner of war at Port Royal, I wrote an official report of the engagement, and received from the Federal authorities a promise that it should be sent with other letters to the Confederate lines. Since my return to the south I find that no such report has been received, and I have therefore the honor of again presenting a detailed account of the operations resulting in the fall of the fort.

Early in the month of February our line of communication with Savannah, which had been threatened for two or three weeks, was completely broken, the enemy having succeeded in getting between us and the city by means of a channel known as Mud river. At the point where this channel joins the Savannah, he placed two heavy batteries, one on the north side of the main river, commanding the north channel, the other upon a marshy island in the middle of the stream, bearing upon the south channel, thus blockading both passages to the fort, and cutting us off effectually from all prospect of receiving relief of any kind from the city. I should add that Mud river is beyond the range of the guns of the fort.

Fortunately our supply of provisions was good, an extra quantity having been sent down to us on the first intimation of danger; so we had nothing to fear on that score. Then, too, the whole garrison had been hard at work for two months in following the directions of General R. E. Lee for the interior defense of the fort. All the casemate doors were protected by blinds of heavy timber — the colonnade in front of the officers' quarters and kitchens torn down, and a traverse of timber and earth substituted — the parade cut up in trenches to catch falling shells, and a traverse and splinter proofs erected at every available point on the rampart, so that we were well protected against shells; and, as experienced engineers had declared it to be impracticable to breach our walls from Tybee island (the nearest point of which is more than double the greatest breaching distance heretofore known, from the fort), I felt fully able to resist any attack that could be made against us. Up to the second week in March we could not see that the enemy on Tybee was making any demonstration towards us, but at that time I began to notice certain changes in the sand hills about two miles from the fort, and my pickets reported almost nightly the noise of wagons and workmen at King's Point, 1,700 yards distant. At this last place, however, we could see nothing whatever; all the work being done at night, and behind a natural parapet or range of sand hills, running parallel with the beach, which completely hid everything from us until a few days before the bombardment, when we opened fire upon a small party of men who showed themselves accidentally. They retired, and we saw no more of working parties.

I did not fire in the direction of the noise at night for various reasons. In the first place our supply of powder, though enough to resist an ordinary naval attack, was far from being sufficient for the prolonged siege I thought before us, and there was no possible chance of getting another pound from any quarter. Again, it would have been but blind work firing out into the darkness without being able to observe the effect of our shots, and at a mark completely hidden from us even in day-light; sound being the only thing to guide our aim.

At an early hour on the morning of the 10th of April, a formal demand was made upon me by Major Gen. Hunter for the surrender of the fort to the forces under his command. I could give him but one answer. The officer who brought the demand returned to Tybee, and at 8 o'clock precisely the firing commenced from the enemy's lower batteries. Then battery after battery took it up, until the whole line had opened ; the fort answering slowly at first, but with more rapidity as the gunners acquired the range of the different batteries.

The firing of the enemy was almost entirely concentrated on the *pan coupé* at the southeast angle of the fort, and it soon became evident to my mind that three of their batteries alone were doing all the work. These three batteries are marked Batteries McClellan, Sigel, and Scott in the small plan annexed to this report. They mounted ten heavy rifled guns (James and Parrott), and four Columbiads, and were so completely masked, that during the most of the first day our men could aim only at the puffs of smoke, there being nothing else to indicate the position of the guns.

About four hours after the action commenced, all of our casemate guns (thirty-two-pounders), at the southeast angle and adjacent to it, were dismounted and useless, and a little later in the day our two Columbiads *en barbette* immediately above, were in the same condition. The firing on both sides continued steadily until dark, when it ceased. I had then an opportunity of ascertaining the amount of damage done to the fort. The southeast angle was in a lamentable condition. The whole wall from the crest of the parapet to the moat was flaked away to the depth of from two to four feet, and as the wall between the arches was originally only about five feet in thickness, weakened too by ventilating flues above the embrasures, it needed but one glance to convince me that a few hours more of such a fire would make a formidable breach. The interior of the fort was also much injured. At eleven o'clock the enemy began a desultory fire which was kept up during the whole night, probably with a view to prevent the garrison from resting, no other end being attained.

At six A. M., on the 11th, the firing again became general, and even more rapid than on the previous day. By ten o'clock a large breach was made in the *pan coupé*, which every shot served to enlarge. At noon the wall of another casemate yielded, and then a new danger sprang upon us. The projectiles from the rifle batteries were passing clear through the breach, sweeping across the parade, and striking against the traverses which protected the north magazine. These traverses were two in number — one of brick immediately covering the magazine door — the other of timber and earth protecting a passage way to the magazine and to a quarter master's store-room. Through this last two or three shells had burst, and their fragments found their way to the quarter master's room only ten or twelve feet from where the magazine door stood open, and the brick-work of the other traverse had been struck repeatedly.

Our condition was now as follows : All but two of the casemate guns bearing upon Tybee were dismounted ; but two of the barbette guns were left that could be brought to bear upon the batteries doing us most injury : the outer wall of two casemates had been entirely shot away, and the two adjoining ones were in a crumbling condition ; the moat was bridged over by the ruins of the wall ; most of our traverses had been riddled by shot, and some of them were no longer serviceable ; the range of officers' quarters and kitchens was badly damaged, and the north magazine was in hourly danger of explosion — our communications being so completely cut off that there was no ground for even the shadow of a hope of relief, while for the same reason no line of retreat was left us.

Under these circumstances I considered the fort as no longer tenable, and believing the lives of the garrison to be my next care, I gave the necessary orders for a surrender, having first conferred with my officers and found them, like myself, impressed with the conviction of the utter hopelessness of a longer struggle.

At half past two o'clock P. M. the white flag was displayed. Firing ceased immediately, and shortly after Brigadier General Q. A. Gillmore — the immediate commander of the troops on Tybee — came over to arrange with me concerning the terms of surrender. These were far from generous, yet illiberal as they were, I have here to record formally and officially a complete breach of faith on the part of the Federals. Article 3d (as will be seen by the originals annexed) distinctly provided that the sick and wounded, under charge of the hospital steward of the garrison, were to be sent up under a flag of truce to the Confederate lines. Months afterwards we heard of these poor fellows at Hilton Head, where some had died, and with one or two exceptions they were all subsequently taken to New York and kept as prisoners with the rest of the garrison until a general exchange was effected.

Our loss was wonderfully small — but four men being dangerously wounded, while some thirteen or fourteen received slight wounds and contusions from flying splinters, etc. This I attribute to the good protection afforded the men by blindages and other interior works, and to the fact that the heaviest fire of the enemy was concentrated upon the southeast angle, even when all of our guns in that quarter had been rendered useless.

My officers and men all behaved most gallantly, fighting after the hope of a successful resistance had left them, with, if possible, more determination than before. It is impossible for me to mention each individual instance of bravery. I can only say that the garrison was all that any commander could wish. It is my pride to have had such men under me.

In conclusion, reviewing the whole action, two facts stand out prominently; 1st, that the walls of an old style fortification could not stand against the new rifle projectiles, and 2d, that the arches of the same fort were able to resist the heaviest vertical fire. Several thirteen-inch mortar shells fell directly

11

upon the ramparts from an immense height, without penetrating beyond the covering of dirt.

The three batteries above mentioned did all the injury, and to them alone may be attributed the fall of Fort Pulaski.

Very respectfully

Your obedient servant,

CHAS. H. OLMSTEAD,

Col. 1st Vol. Reg. of Georgia.

General Q. A. Gillmore the immediate Federal commander on Tybee island, upon the display of the white flag, came over to Cockspur island and was met at the south wharf by Captain F. W. Sims of the Oglethorpe Light Infantry, who conducted him to Fort Pulaski where the following terms of capitulation were finally agreed upon between Colonel Olmstead and himself:

ARTICLE 1. The fort, armament and garrison to be surrendered at once to the forces of the United States.

ART. 2. The officers and men of the garrison to be allowed to take with them all their private effects, such as clothing, bedding, books, etc. This not to include private weapons.

ART. 3. The sick and wounded, under charge of the hospital steward of the garrison, to be sent up under a flag of truce to the Confederate lines; and at the same time the men to be allowed to send up any letters they may desire, subject to the inspection of a Federal officer.

Signed the eleventh day of April, 1862, at Fort Pulaski, Cockspur island, Ga.

CHAS. H. OLMSTEAD,

Col. First Vol. Regt. of Ga., Com'g Fort Pulaski.

Q. A. GILLMORE,

Brig. Gen. Vols., Com'g U. S. forces, Tybee island, Ga.

The garrison surrendered numbered about three hundred and sixty-five men and twenty-four officers, and was composed of the following companies:

The German Volunteers, Capt. Jno. H. Stegin.
The Washington Volunteers, Capt Jno. McMahon.
The Wise Guards, Capt. M. J. McMullen.
The Oglethorpe Light Infantry, Co. B, Capt. F. W. Sims.
The Montgomery Guards, Capt. L. J. Guilmartin.

The following constituted the field and staff:

Col. Charles H. Olmstead, Commanding post.
Maj. John Foley.
Adjutant, M. H. Hopkins.
Quarter Master, Robert Erwin.
Commissary, Robert D. Walker.
Surgeon, J. T. McFarland.
Sergeant Major, Robert H. Lewis.
Quarter Master Sergeant, Wm. C. Crawford.
Ordnance Sergeant, Harvey Lewis.
Quarter Master's Clerk, Edward D. Hopkins.
Commissary Clerk, E. W. Drummond.

All these companies belonged to the First Volunteer Regiment of Savannah, with the exception of the Wise Guards, which was attached to the 25th Georgia. The Reverend Father, Peter Whelan, was also in the fort during the bombardment and at the time of its capture, and by his calm courage and pious ministrations confirmed the hearts and endeared himself to the affections of the entire garrison. A number of colored servants were at the time in attendance upon the officers of the fort.

That Fort Pulaski was gallantly defended is a fact admitted even by the enemy. Its fall must be attributed primarily to the evacuation of Tybee island,

which was at one time occupied by the Confederate
forces. By the 1st Georgia Regulars, Colonel C. J.
Williams, an open sand battery had been constructed —
without bomb-proof, magazine or traverses — mounting
two eight-inch Columbiads, and located near the north
point of the island not far from the martello tower.
This battery was abandoned, and the guns removed
three days after the fall of Port Royal. Two hundred
yards in rear of this battery were stationed a six-
pounder field gun in charge of a detachment of the
Irish Volunteers, Capt. J. B. Read, and four twelve-
pounder mountain howitzers composing the armament
of the Forest City Rangers, Captain (afterwards Colonel) C. H. Way.

The first troops who occupied Tybee island were
ordered there by Col. C. H. Williams, then commanding at Fort Pulaski, on the 13th day of April, 1861,
and consisted of two companies of his regiment (the
1st Georgia Regulars), under the command of Major
(afterwards Brigadier General), Wm. Duncan Smith.
Subsequently his entire regiment garrisoned the island,
until it was ordered to Virginia on the 17th of July,
1861. It was then relieved by the following companies
of the 1st Volunteer Regiment of Georgia, Col. (afterwards Brig. Gen.) H. W. Mercer commanding, viz:
the Republican Blues, Capt. Jno. W. Anderson; the
Forest City Rangers, Capt. C. H. Way; the Irish
Volunteers, Capt. J. B. Read; the City Light Guards,
Capt. S. Y. Levy; and the Telfair Irish Greys, Capt.
Wm. H. Wylly. About the first of August the 25th
Georgia Volunteers, Col. (afterwards Brigadier General), C. C. Wilson commanding, was formed, and
ordered to report for duty to Col. Mercer on Tybee
island. Other companies of the 1st Volunteer Regiment of Georgia constituted a portion of the garrison

of this island during its occupation by the Confederate troops, viz: the Savannah Volunteer Guards, Capt. Jno. Screven; the German Volunteers, Capt. Jno. H. Stegin; and the Phœnix Rifles, Capt. Geo. A. Gordon; but their terms of service were of short duration, and they were assigned to other posts.

This island was held by Confederate troops from about the 13th day of April, to the 13th day of November, 1861. Its evacuation was suggested and hastened by the fall of Port Royal; this disaster rendering the position of the garrison insecure, and liable at any time to capture or isolation by the passage of the enemy's gun-boats through Scull creek and Wright river into the Savannah river. In fact, upon the capture of Port Royal the enemy displayed a lack of enterprise which must be regarded as surprising. Had the advantage there gained been pressed, the entire coast of Georgia, with its every strong-hold, would doubtless have been forced to a surrender. The two eight-inch Columbiads were dismounted by the Forest City Rangers, and were transported to Fort Pulaski where they were subsequently placed in position.

Thus upon the evacuation of Tybee island the approach by the sea was thrown wide open, and the enemy enabled, unopposed, to consummate the erection of those land batteries designed for the reduction of Fort Pulaski. The subsequent operations of the Federals in the Savannah river — a brief history of which has already been presented — resulted in the entire isolation of the fort. Its retention therefore by our forces was, under any circumstances, a mere question of time, the duration of which, under the most favorable auspices, was to be measured by the supplies on hand. Relief was impossible, retreat

impracticable. When therefore the bombardment
commenced, it could be resisted not in the hope of
ultimate success, but only so far as might be necessary to vindicate the honor of the Confederate flag,
and demonstrate the valor of the good and true men
to whom, in this lonely and trying position, the sacred
duty of its defense was entrusted. Impartial history
will pronounce the conduct of the garrison of Fort
Pulaski during this memorable siege and reduction,
brave, deliberate, and worthy of all commendation.

By the nearly three thousand solid shot and shells
fired from the ten and thirteen-inch mortars, and the
eight and ten-inch Columbiads, but little material
damage was done to the fort. To the novel and
unexpected effect of the conical shot and percussion
shells fired from the James and Parrott rifle guns are
due the breaching of the walls, the partial demolition
of the fortification, and the accomplishment of those
results which so soon rendered it untenable. The
proximate cause of the surrender was the imminent
danger of the explosion of the north magazine. As,
however, the concentration of the enemy's fire, and
the cause of this peculiar danger to the north magazine have been fully explained in Col. Olmstead's
official report, it is only necessary to allude to them
here. If the communications of the fort with the
Confederate lines had been uninterrupted, or if there
had been any reasonable hope of their reestablishment, strenuous efforts might have been made to
avert this peril by shifting the powder from this
magazine, or throwing it into the moat, hazardous as
the enterprise must have proved under the bursting
shells of the Tybee batteries. Had there been the
slightest prospect of relief, Fort Pulaski, as in the
case of Fort Sumter, might have been persistently held

until, in its very ruins, it became a stronger work for defensive purposes than when its defiant walls towered in all their symmetry and perpendicularity.

Had there been a single avenue of retreat, this iron storm might have been still longer braved by the gallant garrison, until the crumbling walls of the fortification whose honor and defense were so near their hearts had filled the moat, and no casemate afforded a friendly protection; and then, when the last ray of hope had died out in the gloom of the conflict, that garrison might have been retired from the disabled fort, a train laid to its magazines and fired, and not one brick left upon another to greet the eye of the invader as he gazed upon his barren victory. But, in the absence of all these, in the absolute isolation of the position, so soon as it became evident that the fort could no longer successfully withstand the disintegrating influences of the rifle batteries, that one of its magazines was liable to an explosion which would have involved the annihilation of the entire garrison, and that a further resistance would only protract, not alter the result, it became the duty of the commanding officer, even at the sacrifice of personal pride and the love of glory, to provide for the lives of the brave men under his command. This Col. Olmstead did, and the wisdom and the humanity of his course will be the more surely approved, the more carefully they are considered. With the siege and reduction of Fort Pulaski a new era was inaugurated in the construction and armament of breaching batteries. It is not within the objects of this sketch to enter upon an analysis of the military lessons taught by this memorable event. A bare allusion to three of them, which have been already recorded, may not be deemed irrelevant.

1st. That with heavy rifle guns the practicability of breaching the best constructed brick scarp with satisfactory rapidity at a distance of from 2,300 to 2,500 yards, admits of but very little doubt; that had the enemy possessed the knowledge of their power—as demonstrated by this bombardment—previous to its inception, the eight weeks of laborious preparation for the reduction of Fort Pulaski could have been curtailed to one week, as heavy mortars and Columbiads would have been omitted from the armament of the batteries as unsuitable for breaching at long ranges.

2d. That the minimum distance—say from nine hundred to one thousand yards—at which land batteries have heretofore been considered practically harmless against exposed masonry, must be at least trebled, now that rifled guns have to be provided against.

3d. That mortars are unreliable for the reduction of a good casemated work of small area.[1]

The siege and reduction of Fort Pulaski will be ever regarded as an epoch not only in the history of this war, but also in tracing the practical development of the science of artillery. The impulse which the results there obtained gave to the manufacture of heavy rifled ordnance, and suitable projectiles, was strikingly illustrated during the subsequent operations of the Federals in Charleston harbor, and at other points during the remaining years of the Confederate struggle for independence. Unfortunately for us, we had neither the means nor the facilities for profiting largely by this dearly bought experience.

We cannot conclude this hurried sketch of the isolation, bombardment, and surrender of Fort Pulaski

---

[1] See report of Brig. Gen. Gillmore, U. S. A.

without commemorating an incident of personal daring than which, under the circumstances, nothing could have been more illustrious.

During the severest portion of the second day's bombardment, about eleven o'clock in the forenoon, while the enemy's solid shots were battering the walls, and their shells were bursting above, within, and around the fort scattering their fragments everywhere, the halyards of the garrison flag which floated from the staff planted upon the parapet just over the sally-port, were carried away by a hostile projectile, and the flag fell.

Lieutenant Christopher Hussey of the Montgomery Guards (Capt. Guilmartin), and private John Latham of the Washington Volunteers (Capt. McMahon), immediately sprang upon the parapet — swept at all points by deadly missiles — and, freeing the flag from its fallen and entangled position, bravely bore it to the northeastern angle of the fort, where, rigging a temporary flag-staff on a gun-carriage, they soon again unfolded in proud defiance, amid the smoke and din and dangers of the conflict, the stars and bars of the young Confederacy in whose support they had freely pledged and fearlessly sustained their manliest devotion.

Edward de Almeyda, the gallant standard-bearer of Portugal, in the battle between Ferdinand and Alfonso lost first his right arm, and then his left in the defense of the royal colors, and finally held them firmly between his teeth until he was cut down by his assailants.

In the naval attack upon Fort Moultrie, during the hottest part of the contest, the flag-staff was severed by a cannon ball and the colors fell in the

12

ditch outside of the work. Leaping through one of
the embrasures Jasper caught up that symbol of a
young nation's honor, that emblem of its dearest
hopes, and, lashing it to a sponge-staff, mounted the
parapet where he held it waving proud defiance to the
thundering broadsides of the enemy until another
staff could be procured and placed in position. A
few years later, at the siege of Savannah, this same
brave sergeant while in the act of planting the colors,
which Mrs. Elliott had presented to Colonel Moultrie's
regiment, upon the English redoubt on the Ebenezer
road, received a mortal wound, and fell in the ditch.
When a retreat of the combined French and American assaulting columns was sounded, summoning his
well-nigh exhausted energies for the effort, he succeeded in bearing those colors from the field. "Tell
Mrs. Elliott," said he, as the last life-drops were
ebbing fast from his manly breast, "that I lost my life
supporting the colors which she presented to our
regiment."

In that shock of arms between Harald Hardrada,
and Harold, the brave sea king planting his land-
waster in the midst, and gathering his trustiest
Norsemen in a death ring around it, chanting his
war songs to the last, perished in defense of that
banner.

The devotion of Codrus, the silence of Leæna, the
constancy of Regulus and the self-sacrifice of the
Chevalier d'Assas have all been perpetuated in story
and song; and when the heroic memories of this
momentous struggle for Confederate independence are
garnered up, and the valiant deeds recorded of those,
who in their persons and acts illustrated the virtues
of the truly brave under circumstances of peculiar
peril, and in the hour of supreme danger freely

exposed themselves in defense of the national emblem, let the recollection of this illustrious incident upon the parapet of Fort Pulaski be perpetuated upon the historic page, and the names of these two courageous men be inscribed upon the roll of honor.

CHAPTER IV.

Service of the Battery at various points within the limits of the Military District of Georgia.   One Section on James island.   Battle of Secessionville.

After the fall of Fort Pulaski the Confederate lines were still further contracted by the withdrawal of the pickets from Skidaway island, and the removal of the troops on the Isle of Hope to the main.   In obedience to an order from Brig. Gen. H. W. Mercer commanding, the Chatham Artillery on the 23d of April, 1862, marched from Camp Claghorn, and formed a new encampment on the main, in an old field near Fergerson's Place, distant a little more than a mile from Bethesda.   Present and absent, 152.

We left our beautiful encampment on the Isle of Hope, with its many pleasures and comforts, its growing memories and its happy hours, with unfeigned regret.   The change from its delightful shades to the bare old field — smitten by the warm sun, and frequented by fleas innumerable — was as marked as it was distasteful.   In honor of one of Georgia's most gallant sons, who had recently attracted to himself the admiring gaze of the entire Confederacy for the distinguished part which he sustained at the memorable battle of Shiloh, our new encampment was called Camp Hardee.

The only peculiarity worthy of note connected with this camp, was its proximity to Bethesda, and its Orphan House, an eleemosynary institution rendered famous by the charities of the Countess of Huntington and the eloquence of Whitefield. Over the deserted old field in which our tents were pitched and our battery parked, not a single tree cast its grateful shadow. A solitary live oak stump, converted almost into iron by age and the influences of the changing seasons, stood just in rear of the southern line of tents; a dead mockery of an ancient grove of noble trees whose majestic forms, in years long since numbered with the past, towered in strength and beauty above this now deserted spot. But a few paces from where our guns were parked were seen the traces of a lone Indian mound, almost level with the surrounding plain, in silence and in sadness giving mournful evidence of the former existence of a race whose memory is perpetuated by only a few scattered organic remains fast yielding to the disintegrating influences of the winds and storms of the relentless years which have elapsed since they were expelled from their homes on this low-lying coast.

For six weeks the Chatham Artillery remained encamped at this spot, occupying an isolated position, the monotony of the scene and the term of service interrupted by naught save the daily routine of camp duties, and field drills. Even this place soon assumed an air of comparative comfort. Cook shops and mess arbors were erected by the men. Pleasant shelters were constructed in front of the tents. The dense margin of myrtles towards the creek was cut down and cleared away, so that the cool sea breeze each afternoon, could, without interruption, diffuse its refreshing influences over all. Wells were dug, stables and harness sheds built, and even the pestiferous fleas expelled by the liberal use of myrtle and wild mint profusely scattered under the floorings of the tents.

Locate it where you might, the members of the Chatham Artillery would always, with becoming pride, and with the care and attention characteristic of true gentlemen, see to it that their camp was distinguished above all others by comfort, neatness and cleanliness. Our battery drills at this time were had in a field just in front of Mrs. Huguenin's house, distant from camp some two miles.

April 30th.— During the night of this day we lost a battery horse from disease. This was the first animal which had died since the battery was mounted ; and the fact is mentioned in confirmation of the statement made in the earlier portion of this sketch, that peculiar care and attention were always bestowed upon the battery animals, and that the regulations for general stable police and management were rigidly enforced.

May 1st, 1862, the seventy-sixth anniversary of the company — a day whose annual recurrence had been always hailed with pride, and celebrated with becoming festivities in the history of the Chatham Artillery — was commemorated by the erection of a fine staff for our battery flag, which was run up and saluted with one gun. The scarcity of powder prevented us from indulging in the customary salute.

May 17th.— A reorganization of the company under the provisions of the conscript act was this day perfected, and with the following results :

Captain.	Joseph S. Claghorn, reelected.
Senior 1st Lieutenant.	Charles C. Jones, Jr., " "
Junior " "	John F. Wheaton, elected.
Senior 2d "	Thomas A. Askew, "
Junior " "	Samuel B. Palmer, "

Junior First Lieutenant Julian Hartridge having, prior to the reorganization, been elected a member of the Confederate congress from the first congressional district, had tendered his resignation as an officer of the Battery that he might enter upon the duties of his new position. Senior Second Lieutenant William M. Davidson declined a reelection on account of ill health.

On the night of the 8th of June a section of the Battery, consisting of the Blakely rifle gun and a twelve-pounder bronze howitzer, with full detachments, and everything complete, under command of Senior Second Lieutenant Thomas A. Askew, in obedience to orders, took up the line of march for James island, South Carolina. At the time this order was received, the captain of the Battery was absent on sick leave, and the senior first lieutenant was also absent on detached service.

As this was the first occasion in the history of the company during the war that it was called upon to serve beyond the limits of Georgia, and as this section was the first to encounter the fire of the enemy, it may not be deemed uninteresting or inappropriate to record the names of those constituting the respective detachments.

As already stated, the section was under the command of Lieutenant Askew.

The rifle gun was under the charge of First Sergeant George A. Whitehead. To this gun was assigned the following detachment, viz:

Corporal Miller, Privates Baker, Bilbo, Cole, Crabtree, Demund, Henderson, Theus, Wade and Wylly, and Drivers Heary, Kelly, Kenney and Manion, senior.

Accompanying the twelve-pounder howitzer, in charge of third Sergeant James Miller, was the following detachment, viz:

Corporal Lathrop, Privates Garden, Harmon, Kennedy, Lancaster, Morse, O'Byrne, Richardson, Saussy, (C. H.), Toole and Walker, and Drivers Burke, Coleman, Malone (David) and Smith (Wesley).

This section proceeded by rail to Charleston, was halted at the rail road depot, and thence marched at once to James island, taking position with the Confederate troops there assembled to oppose the advance of the Federals who had effected a landing on that island from the Stono river and were moving upon Charleston. The Confederate lines at that time extended from Fort Pemberton on the Stono river, to Redoubt number one on the outer shore of James island, in rear of Secessionville. That line consisted of a series of detached field works — mutually supporting each other — and armed with siege pieces. That portion of the island in advance of this line being to a certain extent debatable ground, was narrowly watched by our pickets. By rapidly concentrating their forces, and by the unexpected landing at Grimball's point on the Stono, the Federals hoped to find the Confederate forces unprepared, and confidently believed that they would be able to reach the city of Charleston. The want of enterprise on their part, however, and the resistance offered by the comparatively few Confederate troops then on the island, afforded the opportunity for concentration; and when the effort was actually made by the Federals to capture Charleston, it resulted in a signal and disastrous failure. With the skirmishes which antedated the battle of Secessionville, and the movements made to check the advance of the enemy, this section of the Battery was, after its arrival, fully identified.

Some five hundred yards south of the once pleasant and hospitable village of Secessionville, on a narrow tongue of land formed by two creeks, was located

Battery Lamar, constituting the most advanced work on the left of the line held by the Confederates.

It was a simple earth-work, substantially constructed, completely occupying the narrow strip of land, and flanked on each side by creeks and impracticable marshes. It consisted of a plain face looking south in the direction of Battery island and Grimball's point, with an obtuse angle on either flank. The distance to the Stono river is about two miles. The armament of the battery was barely adequate. Subsequently, it will be remembered, when this battery was made the left of the Confederate new lines on James island, it was greatly strengthened, and its armament increased. From the front of Battery Lamar the high ground stretches out fan-shaped to the Stono river. For almost two weeks preceding the memorable battle of Secessionville this battery had been constantly engaged at long range with the Federal batteries, and in checking the advance of the enemy.

On the morning of the 16th of June the Confederate pickets in front of Battery Lamar were driven in before the rapidly advancing assaulting column of the enemy, over three thousand strong, under command of Gen. Stevens. The battery was well nigh taken by surprise; its garrison, few in numbers and worn out by the incessant fatigues of the preceding fortnight, being generally asleep. A discharge of grape, however, at close range, from the eight-inch Columbiad pointed by the gallant Col. J. G. Lamar in person, and a capital shot from the twenty-four-pounder rifle gun, caused such confusion in the head of the charging column that time was afforded to get the infantry supports to the battery in position. A few discharges of canister, and the infantry fire soon drove the enemy bleeding and discomfited from the

13

front of the battery. With commendable gallantry did the Federals advance a second and a third time to the assault, in both instances, however, being compelled to quit the field leaving it strewn with the dead and the dying. Abandoning the direct attack upon the front of the work, the enemy made a flank movement on the right of the battery, and securing a position on the other side of the marsh, and within easy range, poured a well directed, heavy and enfilading musketry fire into the battery which well nigh compelled the cannoneers to abandon their guns, and for the time almost put an end to the engagement. Just at this critical moment, however, Lieut. Col. McEnery, commanding the brave 4th Louisiana Battalion, arrived on the scene of action, and, with the watchword "Remember Butler" upon the lips of his men, restored the fortunes of the day. This flank movement being checked by the Confederate troops rapidly concentrating for the support of Battery Lamar, the enemy sullenly retired, bleeding and defeated at every point, under cover of his gun-boats in the Stono which opened a spiteful but innocuous fire. The section of the Chatham Artillery moved up with the supporting columns of our troops and with them united in pressing the enemy back.

Not many days after this signal and bloody defeat, the Federals wholly abandoned their enterprise and evacuated the island. The section was then ordered to rejoin the battery, which it did on the morning of of the 8th of July—men and battery animals all well, and everything in order.

In February, 1862, Gen. Robert E. Lee, who had for some months been in command of the department of South Carolina, Georgia and Florida, was ordered to Richmond to assume a more extended and important command. The district of Georgia (at this time consisting of two sub-districts, the lower under the command of Brig. Gen. H. W. Mercer, and the upper under the command of Brig. Gen. W. D. Smith), was commanded by Brig. Gen. A. R. Lawton.

Immediately after the battle of Seven Pines Gen. Lawton was ordered to prepare five thousand men to move to Richmond on shortest notice. His telegraphic reply was, "My men to the number designated are ready to march at once, and I earnestly request that I may be ordered to Virginia with them." His application was granted. This magnificent brigade, consisting of the 13th, 26th, 31st, 38th, 60th and 61st Georgia Regiments, was transported as rapidly as the rail road facilities would permit. It numbered 5,700 men, and a better brigade never, in the history of this war, appeared on the field of battle. Upon his arrival at Petersburg Gen. Lawton was ordered to report with his command to Gen. Stonewall Jackson in the valley, and reached him just in time to move rapidly to the attack upon Gen. McClellan's flank at Cold Harbor on the 27th of June, 1862, which resulted in the complete rout of the immense Federal army concentrated for the capture of the Confederate capital. For the first time in its history as an organization, this brigade went into action in this important battle, and there won for itself a reputation, which, in each succeeding conflict to the last days of the Confederate struggle, grew brighter and more illustrious. It was commanded by Gen. Lawton in person in the battles of Cold Harbor, Malvern Hill, Cedar Mountain, and on the first day of the second Manassas. On that day Gen. Ewell lost his leg, and Gen. Lawton was ordered to the command of his division consisting of his brigade and three others, and led it into action on the

second and third days of the second Manassas. He
continued in command of this division at the battle
of Chantilly, at the capture of Harper's Ferry, and
at Sharpsburg where he was borne from the field
seriously wounded. This brigade afterwards sustained
a conspicuous part in the memorable battle of Fre-
dericksburg in December, 1862, where the gallant
adjutant general of the brigade, Captain E. P. Lawton,
late a member of the Chatham Artillery, fell covered
with honor, and lamented by his brave companions
in arms. With that battle closed the campaign of
1862, one of the most illustrious in the annals of this
gigantic war.

As an evidence of the heroic and terrible service
performed by this brigade, it is a matter of historic
record that between the 27th of June and the 13th of
December, 1862, over twenty-two hundred men of its
number were killed and wounded in action!

After Gen. Lawton was disabled, Gen. John B.
Gordon was assigned to the command of this brigade,
and both commander and command, in this heroic
struggle for independence, passed nobly on from one
field of glory to another. Promoted to the command
of a division in the spring of 1864 near the Wilder-
ness, for conspicuous gallantry, this brave and honored
son of Georgia was succeeded in the command by
General C. A. Evans (formerly colonel of the 31st
Georgia), who retained the command of the brigade
until the surrender of the army under General Lee,
which virtually terminated the war.

Upon the departure of Gen. Lawton — who, from the
very first moment, when, by the occupation of Fort
Pulaski Georgia asserted her independence of Federal rule and the resumption of her state sovereignty,
all through the early days of the Confederacy, had,

with zeal and ability, honestly and patriotically devoted his every time and energy to the defense of Georgia, to the accumulation of men and materials, and to the creation of an army just at a period of the greatest doubt, uncertainty and scarcity, and under circumstances peculiarly trying — the command of the district of Georgia devolved upon Brig. Gen. H. W. Mercer, a lineal descendant of the heroic Mercer of revolutionary memory, who, in the darkest hour of his country's hopes — that country a young and feeble nation struggling against fearful odds for its primal deliverance from kingly rule — fell mortally wounded while leading the van at the battle of Princeton.

The cause of the present was not less sacred to truth and liberty than that which had given honor and inspiration to the past; and the worthy son of this honored grandsire from the very inception of our difficulties devoted himself to the best interests of his home and country with a manliness, an intelligence, an earnestness, a singleness of purpose and a purity of action, which alike commanded the respect, and secured the esteem of all who were brought within the sphere of his influence.

At the commencement of the war General Mercer was an honorary member of the Chatham Artillery, having joined that company as an active member in 1836.

The troops at this time remaining within the limits of the military district of Georgia, as nearly as can now be remembered, embraced the following organizations:

Infantry.

25th Regiment Georgia Volunteers, Col. C. C. Wilson.
29th Regiment Georgia Volunteers, Col. Wm. J. Young.
30th Regiment Georgia Volunteers, Col. D. J. Bailey.

54th Regiment Georgia Volunteers, Col. C. H. Way.
10th Georgia Battalion, Maj. J. E. Rylander.
13th Georgia Battalion, Maj. Geo. A. Gordon.
18th Georgia Battalion, Maj. Jno. Screven.
Co. A, Irish Jasper Greens, Capt. M. J. Ford.
Co B, Irish Jasper Greens, Capt. D. O'Connor.
Coast Rifles, Capt. Screven Turner.
City Light Guard, Capt. S. Yates Levy.
Republican Blues, Capt. Jno. W. Anderson.
Emmet Rifles, Capt. A. Bonaud.
Tattnall Guards, Capt. A. C. Davenport.
Irish Volunteers, Capt. J. M. Doherty.

Artillery.

The Chatham Artillery, Light Battery, Capt. J. S. Claghorn.
The Columbus Artillery, Light Battery, Capt. J. S. Croft
The Chestatee Artillery, Light Battery, Capt. T. H. Bomar.
The Jo. Thompson Artillery, Light Battery, Capt. C. R. Hanleiter.
Co. D, 1st Georgia Regulars, Light Battery, Capt. Jacob Read.
Co. A, Oglethorpe Siege Artillery, Capt. Jno. Lama.
Co. B, Oglethorpe Siege Artillery, Capt. J. F. Oliver.

Cavalry.

2d Georgia Battalion, Lieut. Col. Edward Bird.
Hardwick Mounted Rifles, Capt. J. L. McAllister.
Liberty Independent Troop, Capt. W. L. Walthour.
Liberty Guards, Capt. W. Hughes.
Lamar Rangers, Capt. W. Brailsford.
McIntosh Guard, Capt. O. C. Hopkins.
Banks Partizan Rangers, Capt. W. H. Banks.
Randolph Partizan Rangers, Capt. E. C. Anderson, Jr.

In obedience to an order from Brig. Gen. Mercer, on the 10th of June the Chatham Artillery — whose aggregate present and absent at this time was one hundred and fifty-seven—left Camp Hardee and marched to Causton's Bluff, a little more than four miles from the city of Savannah. This new encampment of the company, in honor of the now sainted hero whose sword then gleamed brightest in the Confederate array, and whose brilliant military record furnished examples of conceptions the most startling, endurance the most surprising, action the most remarkable, courage the most wonderful, piety the most unquestioned, devotion to country and liberty the most loyal, and achievements the most important, was called Camp Stonewall Jackson.

The Battery was here parked just to the right of what was afterwards Fort Bartow, upon St. Augustine creek—a convenient location to repulse any attempt of the enemy to move upon Savannah by the way of Wilmington, Whitmarsh, and Oatland islands.

The following is a complete roll of the Chatham Artillery during the month of June, 1862:

Captain Joseph S. Claghorn.
Senior 1st Lieutenant Charles C. Jones, Jr.
Junior 1st Lieutenant John F. Wheaton.
Senior 2d Lieutenant Thomas A. Askew.
Junior 2d Lieutenant Samuel B. Palmer.
1st Sergeant George A. Whitehead, Sergeant Major.
2d Sergeant John A. Lewis.
3d Sergeant James Miller.
4th Sergeant Alexander T. Gray.
5th Sergeant John W. Heidt.
6th Sergeant John Le C. Harden.
7th Sergeant Manuel Molina.
8th Sergeant James M. Hull.
1st Corporal Robert C. Feagin.
2d Corporal Edward S. Lathrop.
3d Corporal James W. McDonald.

4th Corporal Edward F. Neufville.
5th Corporal R. B. King.
6th Corporal George H. Waring.
7th Corporal J. W. McNish.

Privates. Abrahams, J. M.
Baker, W. E. Q.
Baynard, J. S.
Bilbo, John.
Bliss, Lewis.
Bowman, J. H.
Brown, N. B.
Butler, J. F.
Cash, W. J.
Callahan, Daniel.
Cevor, Charles.
Charlton, Robt. M.
Clarke, G. B.
Cole, James.
Cooke, W. R.
Corey, Wm. B.
Crabtree, J. B.
Crawford, R. A.
Davis, J. M.
Deitz, J. G.
Demund, J. H.
Doe, J. F.
Dumas, H. B.
Drummond, E. W.
Elliott, R. H.
Farr, J. M.
Farr, T. C.
Freeman, G. C.
Garden, F. A.
Gaudry, J. B.
Gignilliat, W. R.
Goodwin, C. R.
Gordon, A. H.

Privates. Gray, W. G.
Hackett, E. L.
Harden, W. D.
Harmon, R. F.
Henderson, E. F.
Hendry, G. N.
Holst, C. M.
Howard, W. J.
Hunter, B. M.
Jaudon, W. A.
Johnson, E. C.
Johnston, Geo. H., Jr.
Johnston, J. H.
Jones, S.
Kennedy, R. M. C.
Lampe, M. C.
Lancaster, J. S. F.
Law, S. S.
Lyon, J. H.
Magill, J. W.
Mallette, P. H.
Marshall, T. B.
McAlpin, J. W.
Miller, T. R.
Mitchell, S. W.
Morel, C. T.
Morse, A. E.
Myers, F.
Mills, E.
Norwood, W. G.
O'Bryne, J. L.
Patten, W. C.
Philips, C.

Privates.
Pond, T. G.
Richardson, J., Jr.
Robert, C.
Rossignol, L. H.
Saddler, W. D.
Saussy, J. R.
Saussy, C. H.
Silva, A. W.
Silva, J. S.
Simpson, J. M.
Smith, H., Jr.

Privates.
Stibbs, H.
Sollie, F. C.
Theus, T. N.
Tenbroeck, J. B.
Toole, A. V.
Turner, G.
Wade, W.
Walker, W. A.
Ward, H. T.
West, A. M.
Wylly, W. D.

Artificer. Holt, A.

Artificer. McLane, H.

Drivers.
Burke, J.
Browne, W.
Burns, Michl.
Broderick, R.
Callahan, M.
Cashin, P.
Christman, J.
Clarke, J.
Coleman, J.
Couroy, J.
Cooper, J.
Craven, W.
Dunn, T.
Egan, M.
Garrett, C.
Gillespie, T.
Golden, J.
Haggerty, M.
Heery, J.
Hughes, J.
Kelly, M.
Kenney, T.
Lammon, W. H.

Drivers.
Leary, J.
Lynch, C.
Maguire, J. C.
MacAvaddy, M.
McTygue, J.
McVeigh, T.
Malone, David.
Malone, Patrick.
Manion, J., Jr.
Manion, J., Snr.
Miller, J.
Molloy, P.
Myler, W.
O'Brien, P., Jr.
O'Brien, P., Snr.
O'Brien, M.
Rafferty, J.
Siney, P.
Slammon, M.
Smith, W.
Tearney, J.
Tomlinson, A.
Williamson, J.

July 26th, 1862.— This day eighteen members of the company were discharged under the operation of the conscript act of the Confederate states, which, among other provisions, authorized the president of the Confederate states to call out and place in the military service for three years — unless the war should

14

sooner end—all white men, residents of the Confederacy, between the ages of eighteen and thirty-five
not legally exempt from military service; and extended the term of enlistment of all those soldiers in
the field between the ages specified, to three years
from the date of their original enlistment, unless the
war was sooner terminated.

Congress, in the passage of this act, added but
another to the long series of blunders which characterized its short-sighted legislation.   Such were the
evil influences of the act, to such an extent did its
practical operation weaken the armies of the Confederacy—already far too small to cope with the
accumulating hosts which the·enemy from without its
own vast territory and from the floating population of
the world was sending to the field—that an order was
issued by the secretary of war directing that all
enlisted men, who under the provisions of this act
would be entitled to a discharge on the 16th of July,
1862, should be retained in service for ninety days
longer.   This order, although in contravention of the
legislation of the Confederate congress, was based
upon the necessities of the country, which at that
moment needed in the tented field every man capable
of bearing arms who could possibly be spared from
other and important duties, and demanded a willing
obedience from all who had the good of the nation at
heart, and held the success of our arms and the
triumph of our cause at such an eventful epoch
superior to the claims of personal ease and private
interests.   The term of enlistment of the members
of the Chatham Artillery did not expire until August
1st, 1862.   In their anxiety, however, to avail themselves of the provisions of this act, and to obtain the
discharge from service therein provided, some of

the members of the company, exempt under the terms of the act, employed counsel to sue out writs of *habeas corpus*.

A conflict between the civil and military authorities seemed inevitable. The order of the war department was imperative, and if enforced would render practically inoperative any process of the courts. Gen. Mercer was at first inclined, looking to the good of the service, to hold the applicants and disregard any judicial action in the premises. Pending, however, the decision of the *habeas corpus* cases, Lieut. Jones, who had been detailed for that purpose, returned from Camp Randolph, near Calhoun, Georgia, with thirty-eight conscripts—a number more than sufficient to supply the places of all members of the battery over thirty-five and under eighteen years of age who would be entitled to a discharge under the operation of the conscript act. Upon proper representation of this fact the applicants were discharged, and the anticipated conflict between the military authorities and the civil courts was avoided.

The exemption from military service thus procured was of short duration; for congress perceiving its error, and appreciating more fully the wants of the army, by subsequent legislation placed these exempts in the field where of right they belonged.

The company cheerfully acquiesced in the conscript act, and realized the fact that it was in for the war.

As the summer months progressed, this locality proved exceedingly unhealthy. Situated as was the camp in the vicinity of the rice fields, low grounds, and brackish marshes of the Savannah river, and therefore in the midst of a truly malarial region, the men suffered so generally and so severely from fevers, that at one time there were scarcely cannoneers enough in camp to perform guard duty, or drivers to attend to stable duties. Several deaths occurred, and the removal of the company became a matter of necessity.

Accordingly, on the 7th of August, by permission of the brigadier general commanding, the Battery marched to White bluff and there went into permanent camp. The change was most grateful. We were again remanded to the pleasures and the comforts of the salt water and pure sea air; but the seeds of disease still lingered in the systems of not a few of the men, and, in many instances, months elapsed before the malarial poisons imbibed at Camp Jackson were thoroughly eradicated.

Our tents were pitched in a beautiful pine grove, within sight of the river and the wide-spreading salt marshes over which the cool sea breezes came each afternoon with their health-bringing influences. Stables, black-smith and harness shops, cook houses and cabins were soon constructed, and the encampment with all its comforts and conveniences presented the appearance of a model camp, well-nigh equalling the attractions and the pleasures of Camp Claghorn.

This camp was known as Camp Ashby — a token of respect to the memory of the gallant cavalry colonel whose early and dashing exploits invested his name almost with that attractive romance which gave dignity and honor to the most chivalrous passages at arms upon which the student of the past delights to linger.

The Battery numbered, aggregate present and absent, one hundred and sixty-five men. The battery animals had been carefully trained and were in beautiful order. All the appointments of the battery were excellent. Nothing was wanting except guns of greater power. Such was the proficiency of the drill of the cannoneers, that there was nothing in the schools of the soldier, the piece, and the battery, which could not be promptly, accurately, and handsomely executed. Strict and constant attention was bestowed upon both park and field drills. Upon a small field adjacent to the encampment the parade was formed each Sabbath morning for inspection and review, while the regular battery drills were conducted in an open field, well suited to the purpose, just opposite the White Bluff church on the Vernon shell road.

On the 14th of October, First Lieut. C. C. Jones, Jr. was commissioned as lieutenant colonel of artillery and ordered to report for duty to Brig. Gen. Mercer, by whom he was announced as chief of artillery, and ordered to the command of the light batteries in the military district of Georgia.

On the 12th of December, Captain Joseph S. Claghorn resigned the command of the company, and subsequently accepted the appointment of lieutenant colonel, and ordnance officer upon the staff of Major Gen. Gustavus W. Smith, commanding the Georgia militia, and the state forces.

Too much credit cannot be awarded to Captain Claghorn for the industry, care, and ability which he had evinced in placing this light battery in the field, and in bringing it up to its present standard of drill, discipline, and general excellence. His patriotic labors in behalf of his company — the interest which he ever manifested in its welfare — the intelligence with which he discharged every duty devolving upon him — the happy influence which he exerted over his men — the pride which he at all times cherished in his battery — and the zeal he exhibited in promoting its every advantage will be always remembered with peculiar pleasure in the history of the Chatham Artillery.

The vacancies thus caused were filled by the promotion of Junior First Lieutenant John F. Wheaton to the captaincy, of Senior Second Lieutenant Thomas A. Askew to the senior first lieutenancy, of Junior Second Lieutenant Samuel B. Palmer to the junior first lieutenancy, and by the election of Sergeant Major George A. Whitehead to the senior second lieutenancy, and of Sergeant George N. Hendry to the junior second lieutenancy.

These officers retained their respective positions in the battery to the close of the war.

During the most of his subsequent term of service, Lieut. Whitehead was on detached duty as adjutant of the light batteries in the military district of Georgia.

On the 24th of October the Battery marched to Coffee bluff to resist a threatened landing by the enemy. After firing a few shots, however, the Federal gun-boats retired. The Battalion of the Savannah Volunteer Guards, the 4th Louisiana Battalion, and Captain Read's Battery of Light Artillery were also concentrated at this point.

Nothing of peculiar interest marks the history of the company during the remainder of the year. The morning report for the 31st of December, 1862, shows an aggregate present and absent of one hundred and forty-six men.

On the 8th of January, 1863, the light batteries stationed in the vicinity of Savannah were assembled upon the city commons in rear of the jail by Lieut. Colonel Jones commanding, for parade, inspection, and review by Brig. Gen. Mercer commanding the

military district of Georgia. This was the first time
in the history of Georgia that a battalion of light
artillery was ever concentrated and manœuvred within
her borders. About four hundred men, three hundred
battery animals, and twenty-six field pieces were present upon this parade; and the fact is worthy of com-
memoration, that during the entire inspection, review
and subsequent parade there was not the slightest de-
rangement in the movements of the respective batteries.
To the Chatham Artillery, by common consent, was
awarded the highest commendation for its military
appearance, accuracy of drill and general proficiency.
The companies assembled on this occasion were the
Chatham Artillery, Capt. Wheaton; the Terrel Artillery, Capt. Dawson (Lieut. Brooks commanding); the
Regular Light Battery, Capt. Read (Lieut. Guerard
commanding); the Columbus Artillery, Capt. Croft,
and the Chestatee Artillery, Capt. Bomar (Lieut.
Hendricks commanding).

During this year, and until the Battery was ordered
to James island, it was, in conjunction with the other
light batteries in the district, regularly drilled by the
lieutenant colonel commanding in the battalion drill for
light artillery prepared by Major Robert Anderson
of the United States army. These drills were peculiarly interesting, and were conducted with great
spirit. The effect was most salutary, and the generous rivalry thus engendered was productive of good
among the respective batteries concentrated for the
defense of Savannah. The fact should be here noted,
that during the continuance of the entire war the
light artillery companies of the military district of
Georgia were marked by a proficiency in drill, and a
general excellence of equipment which distinguished
them above others in the department.

CHAPTER V.

Two sections of the Battery on the Great Ogeechee River. History
of the naval attacks upon Fort McAllister, and of its final capture
by assault.

On the 30th of January, 1863, Lieut. Whitehead
with two detachments from the Battery in charge of
a three and a half-inch Blakely gun, and a twelve-
pounder rifled gun, was ordered to take post on
the Great Ogeechee river within supporting distance of Fort McAllister. On the same day Lieut.
Askew with a section of twelve-pounder howitzers,
and two detachments, numbering in the aggregate
twenty-seven men, marched to Kings Bridge on the
Great Ogeechee river, and there remained for the
protection of that important communication, with
instructions to dispute vigorously the advance of the
enemy in case they forced the passage of the river in
front of Fort McAllister.

Three days before the fort had been severely bombarded by the enemy, and there was every indication
that the attack would be renewed at an early moment
and with greater determination. Light field works
had been thrown up at the most advantageous points
along the banks of the river between the fort and the
rail road crossing of the Great Ogeechee swamp and
river, with a view to impeding, and if possible, successfully resisting their ascent of the river in case the
Federal gun-boats should pass the battery at Genesis
point. Behind these, ramps and platforms had been

arranged for light artillery. To the specific duty of occupying these positions in case the emergency arose, the section of the battery under the command of Lieut. Whitehead was assigned, with general orders, in the event of a renewal of the naval attack upon the fort, to keep in its vicinity, and be prepared to advance rapidly to repulse any attempted landing from the vessels.

Sergeants Garden and Mitchel accompanied this section as chiefs of pieces, and Corporals Walker and Baker as gunners. One hundred and twenty-five rounds of ammunition were carried to the piece, and the entire equipment of the section was complete. The first position selected and occupied during the memorable bombardment of the 1st of February, was some three-quarters of a mile above the fort in full view of the operations of that historic engagement.

The name of Fort McAllister will ever remain famous in the martial annals of Georgia, and history will delight to dwell with peculiar pride and satisfaction upon the valor which defended and the patriotism which glowed within its walls. Although the changing seasons have already spread the mantle of decay above its desolated magazines, and wild flowers are blooming in its vacant chambers, the memories which it has so nobly given to the great cause of right and liberty will survive, and be ardently cherished so long as truth has an advocate or heroism an admirer.

This fort constituted the right of the exterior line of defenses designed and held for the protection of Savannah. Situated on the lowest high ground on the right bank of the Great Ogeechee river, at Genesis point, it effectually commanded the channel of that river, and afforded ample security against any ordinary naval force intended for the destruction of the

15

rail road bridge, and the disorganization of the important rice plantations in the neighborhood. From the time of its construction—which was coeval with our earliest coast defenses—to the day of its capture on the 13th of December, 1864, it subserved purposes most conducive to the general welfare, and on various occasions gallantly repulsed repeated and well directed naval attacks by the enemy. No name is more proudly remembered on our coast than that of this small earth-work near the mouth of the Great Ogeechee.

The first attack sustained by this fort occurred on the 29th of June, 1862. It was then in an unfinished condition, with an armament of only one forty-two-pounder, and five thirty-two-pounder guns. Its garrison consisted of the DeKalb riflemen, under the command of Capt. Alfred L. Hartridge. Four Federal gun-boats—one a side wheel steamer, and the other three, propellers—armed with eleven-inch Dahlgren and rifle guns, composed the attacking fleet. Over seven hundred shots were fired by the enemy, and the action continued for two hours and a quarter. The Confederates replied slowly and carefully, using their guns only when the vessels ventured within range. For the most part the bombardment was maintained at a distance beyond the reach of the battery of the fort, the rifle guns of the enemy giving them under such circumstances a decided advantage. One of the Federal vessels was struck. The quarters in the fort were considerably damaged, and the forty-two-pounder gun was disabled during the engagement. Only two men of the garrison were wounded. Fort McAllister was on this occasion deliberately and ably defended, and the enemy here encountered a repulse which was but the prelude to others more signal.

On the 2.1 of November of the same year, Capt. A. Bonaud, while in an open boat engaged in reconnoitering the exact position of the Federal fleet, and when within some twelve hundred yards of one of the vessels, was discovered. The enemy at once opened fire upon him, and dispatched two barges in pursuit. This pursuit was maintained until the barges were drawn under the fire of the fort, before which they retreated precipitately. One of the gun-boats approached and bombarded the fort at long range for some time, but without causing any injury. On this occasion the garrison consisted of the Emmett Rifles.

Seventeen days afterwards, two gun-boats and one mortar boat commenced shelling Fort McAllister at 8 o'clock, A. M., and continued the bombardment until three o'clock in the afternoon, throwing several hundred projectiles. They kept studiously beyond the range of the guns of the battery, only at intervals venturing near enough to draw the fire of the fort, and at no time approaching within a mile. Twelve shots only were fired from the fort, one of which took effect upon the foremost vessel. Three men of the garrison—at that time consisting of the Republican Blues, and the Emmett Rifles—were wounded. Lieut. George W. Anderson was in command. The battery of the fort had previously been increased by the addition of an eight-inch Columbiad.

On the morning of the 27th of January, 1863, the Federal iron-clad Montauk, accompanied by the gun-boats Wissehicken, Seneca and Dawn, the mortar schooner C. P. Williams, and the tug Daffodil, advanced up the river, and at half-past seven o'clock opened fire upon the fort. The Montauk, armed with one fifteen-inch, and one eleven-inch Dahlgren gun, took up a position nearly abreast of the battery and in close proximity to the obstructions extending across the river in front of the fort. For five hours and a half, assisted by the other vessels at longer range, did she hurl her enormous projectiles against the sand parapet, and explode them within the parade of this heroic little fort, whose heaviest guns, although handled with skill and determination, were powerless against her thick iron-sides and heavily plated turret. Despite this formidable demonstration and the enormous expenditure of shot and shell on the part of the enemy, the damage done to the fort was repaired before morning, and not a single casualty occurred among the members of the garrison. Major John B. Gallie commanded the fort during this bombardment, and the guns principally used in replying to the enemy were the eight-inch Columbiad, and a rifle thirty-two-pounder gun which had been recently added to the battery. The men, one and all, as on previous and subsequent occasions, exhibited in the discharge of every duty devolved upon them a deliberation and a courage worthy of every commendation.

To this bombardment remarkable historical interest attaches, because, on this occasion, a *fifteen-inch gun was first used in the effort to reduce a shore battery;* and the ability of properly constructed sand parapets to resist the effect of novel projectiles, far surpassing in weight and power all others heretofore known, was fairly demonstrated. To the honor of this little fort, and to the praise of its heroic defenders let these facts be recorded and perpetuated.

As at Fort Pulaski the problem of the reduction of masonry walls at unusual ranges by rifle guns was solved to the surprise of many, and in contradiction of accepted theories, so at Genesis point the value of sand parapets was fully substantiated in the face of guns of novel calibre and power.

Thus upon the coast of Georgia two military lessons were first learned, the value of which proved of prime importance in the subsequent conduct of the war, lessons which caused, and must continue to render necessary most essential modifications in the construction of permanent fortifications and the erection of coast defenses.

The result of this iron-clad attack upon Fort McAllister greatly encouraged the spirit of its gallant defenders, and diminished the confidence of the enemy in the abilities of their vaunted vessels.

Not satisfied, however, with the experiment, mortified at the results of their repeated attacks, and resolved upon the reduction of this heroic fort, the enemy about half-past seven o'clock on Sabbath morning, the first of February, renewed the attack, and for some six hours directed against Fort McAllister a fierce and terrific bombardment. The thunders of those hostile guns strangely marred the stillness of the holy day, and with harsh discord invaded even the sanctuaries of the living God. Fervently did the prayers of the assembled worshippers within the respective churches in the city of Savannah ascend on that day to the God of battles in behalf of fathers, husbands, and brothers who were gallantly passing through this fearful ordeal. Those prayers were answered, and the enemy for the fifth time was compelled to retire from the contest, vanquished and discomfited. In this bombardment the iron-clad Montauk was assisted by four gun-boats and one mortar boat.

The following dispatches, sent by Col. Robert Anderson to Gen. Mercer at Savannah during the progress of the engagement, contain in a few words its history, and truthfully express the conduct and the determination of the brave men to whom were entrusted the defense of this important position and the honor of the Confederate flag:

WAYS STATION, Feb. 1, 8.10 A. M.

A Yankee iron-clad is anchored about two hundred yards from the obstructions. Four gun-boats and one mortar boat are opposite to, and two miles from the battery. The firing is very rapid.

Major Gallie has just been killed, and one of the men buried in the sand.

Our parapet in front of the eight-inch gun is entirely demolished, though the detachment is still at the gun. One of our thirty-two-pounders is disabled.

We will hold the battery to the last extremity, and blow it up before we will surrender. The attack is severe, but the men are in fine spirits.

8.30 A. M.—The fog deceived me as to the distance. Instead of being two hundred yards from the obstructions, the iron-clad is between a quarter and a half mile from them.

9.20 A. M.—The iron-clad has been struck several times, and is slowly falling down the river, though she is still within a thousand yards of the battery.

The battery has received no further damage.

The garrison is in fine spirits, and everything working beautifully.

Two more men have been slightly wounded.

1 P. M.—The garrison, after a most gallant and determined resistance, have driven off the enemy.

The behavior of the officers and men was noble.

The damage to the works can be repaired in about two hours.

Our loss is: Major Gallie killed, and seven privates wounded— none seriously.

Early in the action Major Gallie commanding the fort was wounded by a shell, and upon its explosion almost buried in the sand. Gallantly refusing to retire from the post of danger, he continued passing from gun to gun, encouraging his men and directing the fire of the battery. Not long afterwards, while in the chamber of one of the thirty-two-pounder guns, the piece was struck by a fifteen-inch shell, and by its left trunnion Major Gallie was hit in the head and instantly killed. Upon his death the command devolved upon Captain George W. Anderson. In the language of one of the public journals:

With one gun disabled, their beloved commander gone, and another gun exposed to the open fire of the enemy, victory on the part of the assailants seems but a question of time; but the command has devolved upon one who has never learned the lesson of surrendering. For five hours the fort, thus exposed, was subjected to a continued and heavy bombardment not only from the iron-clad—throwing immense fifteen-inch and eleven-inch shells and solid shot, and at times grape — but also from the gun-boats and mortar-boat, which, at a distance beyond the reach of our guns, with their rifled cannon threw projectile after projectile within the very parade of the fort. The service of the guns in the fort was deliberate; no excitement, no idle waste of ammunition, each piece being well aimed, and the solid shot from the eight-inch Columbiad and the forty-two-pounder gun again and again striking full against the turret of the Monitor. It is a fact worthy of note — one which should be carefully preserved in the historical recollections of this war — that on the present occasion was used for the [1] first time in actual combat a fifteen-inch gun. A proper appreciation of the immense weight and force of the projectile hurled from this enormous engine of war, casemated too in an iron turret whose sides are twelve inches in thickness, supported by an eleven-inch

---

[1] This was not the *first*, but the *second* time that a fifteen-inch gun had been employed in the effort to reduce a shore battery. The first time it was used in this manner, was during the bombardment of Fort McAllister, on the 27th of January, five days before.

gun, will best enable us to realize the dangers which surrounded the garrison behind the open sand parapets of Fort McAllister, and, to some extent at least, sufficiently to admire the heroism which prompted them in such an exposed position hour after hour to stand to their guns, and without the slightest fear maintain the unequal contest. Both of the flags, which were flying from the bow and stern of this iron monster, were entirely shot away by the well directed aim of our guns, and although one of them fell full upon the deck of that vessel, not an officer or man on board was found brave enough to come forth from his secure retreat within the iron turret, and lift from their trailing, fallen position those stars and stripes, once the symbol of a great people's honor — now the national emblem of the Abolition hosts — a flag which never trailed so long as Southern hearts swelled in honor of the liberties it was designed to protect, so long as Southern arms were nerved in its defense.

Contemplate for one moment the contrast here presented by the opposing forces: on the one hand you see the Abolition troops, encircled by all the invulnerability which Yankee ingenuity is so apt to contrive for the protection of human life, skulking behind and within their iron-casemated turret, and not daring to expose themselves even for one moment to the fire of the fort, to lift from its fallen, prostrate position that flag which they profess so much to admire and love, a flag which they worship with more reverence than the God of truth, justice and honor.

On the other hand, in open view, you have the brave garrison of that little fort — firm as a rock — undaunted amid the hailstorm of shot, shell and grape which for hours burst above and around them — exposed to every danger, yet recking none — with more than Spartan heroism maintaining the defense of their position, and illustrating in examples of living light the true manhood of southern soldiery armed in the holy cause of a nation's honor, of personal right, and of common justice.

Does the picture suggest no idea of a difference of races? Are we not reminded of the fact that the present is but another illustration of the truth that the Almighty has, in his own providence caused two separate and distinct races — distinct in feature, in language, in conceptions of honor, and of courage — to spring up on this continent, who can no more be again united than can the pure bright waves that dance along our coast be made to mingle in unison with the nauseous oils of a Nantucket whale ship?

But even the famous iron-clad cannot longer withstand the repeated and well directed fire of Fort McAllister. Her turret ceases to revolve, and this behemoth slowly drops down the stream, far out of the reach of the guns of our battery, where she has lain ever since, loth to renew the conflict. Thus has the experiment with the famed iron-clads been made, and it is a proud satisfaction to reflect that to Georgia belongs the honor of successfully demonstrating the fact that, by the blessing of God, an open sand battery, supported by her brave sons, can withstand a bombardment by a first class iron-clad, armed with enormous fifteen inch guns. The lesson of the past gives renewed assurance of the future.

The death of Major Gallie was a source of especial sorrow to the Chatham Artillery, of which company he was an honorary member at the time. For many years his associations with that company had been of the closest character, and his attachment for, and his interest in that organization were the most cordial and abiding. He had successively filled every office in the gift of his admiring Chatham Artillerymen, to whom the recollection of his many virtues, and of his heroic death will ever remain peculiarly precious. The following tribute to his memory, penned by a friend a few days after his lamented fall — if here repeated — will not be deemed out of place by those who knew and esteemed him while in life, and who will delight to perpetuate the remembrance of the true friend, the valuable citizen, the upright man, and the pure patriot:

16

The late Major John B. Gallie, who was killed in the performance of duty as commandant of Genesis Point Battery when
it was attacked by the enemy on Sunday last, was born at Dor-
noch, Scotland, on the 1st day of July, 1806, and was consequently fifty-six years and seven months old at his death.   At
the age of sixteen, being possessed of a good constitution, a
useful education, and correct habits and principles inculcated
both by precept and example, he determined to seek his fortunes
in the western hemisphere.   Actuated no doubt by the choice
of location made by the agricultural population of his native
country, who were inhumanly banished *en masse* by the Countess,
afterwards the Duchess of Sutherland, he arrived in Nova Scotia,
and remained in the British North American provinces for
upwards of seven years.   Afterwards he spent a year in New
Orleans, but for upwards of thirty years he has been a resident
of this city, during which he was engaged in various pursuits,
having been for a long period treasurer of the iron steam boat
company, and was at the time of his death a partner in the firm
of J. R. Wilder & Gallie, of this city.   Formerly he was inter-
ested to a considerable extent in the shipping and steamers of
this port, as well as internal improvements, and was ever ready
to hold out a helping hand to public enterprises calculated to
benefit this city.

He always evinced a strong partiality for military life, and
was for many years a member of the Chatham Artillery, in
which he served in all grades from the lowest to the highest.
When it became evident that a separation was about to take
place between the north and south, he was mainly instrumental
in getting up the Savannah Artillery, a fine body of men, who
elected him their commander; but, unfortunately he did not
remain long at its head, and the company was disbanded.   He
then raised and commanded a battalion of artillery in the service of the state, which was disbanded by the operation of the
conscript law of April last, and he had almost succeeded in rais-
ing a battalion for Confederate service, when orders were issued
from the adjutant general's office at Richmond which prevented
his doing so.   Through the recommendation of Brig. Gen.

Mercer, he was appointed major in the Confederate service, and was immediately assigned to the command of the post in the defense of which he yielded up his life.

The deceased was so long and favorably known in this community that panegyric is useless; but it was only by the very few to whom he gave his entire confidence that his sterling worth could be properly appreciated. Whenever he was in doubt, he never failed to take counsel of them, after which his determination was taken and he was immovable, and always did what he believed to be right. He was a fond husband and father, an indulgent master, a true friend, and kind and obliging to all. A pure patriot, a brave man, and a sincere but unostentatious Christian, he has laid down his life for his adopted country, and has gone, accompanied by the grief of his heart-broken and much bereaved family, and the sincere sorrow of this entire community, "where the wicked cease from troubling and the weary are at rest."

This signal victory was made the subject of the following congratulatory general orders by General Beauregard commanding the department of South Carolina, Georgia, and Florida.

HEAD QUARTERS, DEPARTMENT of S. C., GA. and FLA.,
Charleston, S. C., Febuary 6th, 1863.

GENERAL ORDERS, No. 23.

The commanding general announces to the forces, with satisfaction and pride, the results of the recent encounter of our battery at Genesis Point, Georgia, with an iron-clad of the monitor class — results only alloyed by the life-blood of 'the gallant commander, the late Major John B. Gallie.

For hours the most formidable vessel of her class hurled missiles of the heaviest calibre ever used in modern warfare at the weak parapet of the battery, which was almost demolished; but, standing at their guns as became men fighting for homes, for honor, and for independence, the garrison replied with such effect as to cripple and beat back their adversary, although clad in impenetrable armor, and armed with fifteen and eleven-inch guns, supported by mortar boats, whose practice was of uncommon precision.

The thanks of the country are due to this intrepid garrison, who have thus shown what brave men may withstand and accomplish, despite apparent odds.

Fort McAllister will be inscribed on the flags of all the troops engaged in the defense of the battery.

By command of General Beauregard.

Signed   THOMAS JORDAN,

Chief of Staff.

The section of the Chatham Artillery under the command of Lieut. Whitehead — although present in the immediate neighborhood — took no active part in the engagement, there existing no necessity for the use of field guns. At this time the other section of the battery, Lieut. Askew commanding, was stationed on the Great Ogeechee near the crossing of the Atlantic and Gulf rail road.

On the 28th of February the Nashville, in attempting to pass down the Great Ogeechee in order to run the blockade with a cargo of some seven hundred bales of cotton, besides a considerable quantity of resin and tobacco, got aground on a sand bar about a mile distant from Fort McAllister. Seeing her situation, the Montauk moved up to within three-quarters of a mile of the Nashville, and after firing a number of shots, finally succeeded with her shells in igniting that vessel and totally destroying her. The fort opened upon the iron-clad, but failed to drive her away or to cause any apparent damage. This fire was returned by three wooden gun-boats and by a mortar boat, at long range. No casualties occurred on the Confederate side. After the destruction of the Nashville, the Federal vessels retired to their anchorage below the fort. At the time of her loss, the name of this vessel had been changed to the Rattlesnake. Letters of marque had been obtained for her, and she carried a battery consisting of one thirty-two-pounder, and one twenty-four-pounder gun. During this attack upon the Nashville, one of the torpedoes in the Great Ogeechee which had been placed in position below the fort, was exploded by the Montauk while passing over it. It is believed that this vessel was injured by the explosion, as it took no active part in the subsequent bombardment of the fort a few days afterwards.

The seventh, and by far the most powerful attack upon Fort McAllister was made on the 3d of March. Chagrined at their former defeats, the enemy appeared resolved on this occasion to compass the destruction of this heroic and already famous battery, and accordingly concentrated for its annihilation the following formidable fleet:

The Passaic—a monitor—commander Drayton, armed with one fifteen-inch, and one eleven-inch Dahlgren gun.

The Patapsco—a monitor—commander Ammen, carrying one fifteen-inch Dahlgren, and one two-hundred-pounder Parrott.

The Montauk—a monitor—commander Worden, with a battery of one fifteen-inch and one eleven-inch Dahlgren.

The Nahant—a monitor—commander Downs, armed with one fifteen-inch and one eleven-inch Dahlgren.

The Peira, Captain Tarbox, and two other thirteen-inch mortar schooners.

To complete the list, the gun-boats Wissahickon, Down, Sebago, Seneca and Flambeau, were present, and together with the Montauk constituted a reserve.

Against this array the fort could oppose only its former guns, strengthened by the addition of a ten-inch Columbiad. The Federals evidently contemplated a successful issue, as General Seymour was present and had troops on steam boats ready to land and take possession of the fort so soon as the brave defenders should be driven from their guns by the terrible storm of enormous projectiles soon to burst in awful grandeur above, around, and within the limited confines of this small earth-work.

The bombardment was commenced about forty minutes after eight o'clock, A. M., by the mortar boats stationed nearly two miles below the fort, and beyond the range of its guns. So soon as this fire had been fairly opened, the monitor fleet slowly advanced toward the fort, the Passaic taking the lead, the Patapsco and the Nahant following. While coming into position the Confederates opened upon the Passaic with ten-inch solid shot, and repeatedly struck her. So soon as the iron-clads had selected an anchorage, the engagement became general, and was continued with but slight intermission until half-past four o'clock, P. M., when the monitors retired — the mortar boats keeping up the bombardment until day-break the next morning. It was the design of the enemy to renew the attack on the morning of the 4th, but when, upon examination, it was discovered that all the damages sustained by the sand parapets of the fort had been, during the night, fully repaired, and that Fort McAllister was to all appearances as prepared for the conflict as it was when the first gun had been fired, the Federal commander recognizing his inability to reduce the work, or to strike terror into the hearts of the heroic garrison, retired his fleet and abandoned the effort; thus according to the brave defenders of Fort McAllister a most

signal and crowning victory — a victory which takes
rank with the proud achievements of this memorable
war — a triumph which will be always mentioned in
the history of this eventful period with especial pride —
a triumph which settled the question of the ability of
properly constructed sand batteries to withstand prolonged and formidable bombardment from the most
powerful iron-clads in the Federal navy.

It is admitted by the enemy that the Passaic was
struck thirty-one times, and once by a ten-inch solid
shot within three inches of her port-hole. The Nahant and Patapsco were also frequently hit. Early
in the action it was ascertained by the Confederates
that the projectiles from the guns of the fort were too
light to penetrate the armor of the iron-clads, or to
cause material injury to them; accordingly the revo-
lutions of the turrets were narrowly watched, and, as
a general rule, our guns were fired only when there
was a chance of entering the open ports. In the fort
everything was characterized by deliberation, and
consummate bravery.

The following spirited account of this historic engagement is borrowed from the *Savannah Republican*
of the 11th of March, 1863. It contains some trivial
errors as to the names and armaments of the Federal
vessels engaged, which the reader will readily correct:

This remarkable engagement is deserving a more extended
notice than it has heretofore received at the hands of the press.
That one of the most terrible conflicts of the revolution should
be disposed of in a few lines of telegraphic report, embracing
only its result, is not just to the noble and heroic spirits who
on that memorable occasion defended successfully the soil of
Georgia against an armament, which, in force and terror, is
without a parallel. The brigadier general commanding the
department has, in part, supplied the omission by his compli-

mentary order to be found on the second page of this paper. There are other facts though, embracing the entire details of the engagement, which should be put on record as part of the history of this unnatural and sanguinary war. True it was a bloodless battle so far as our forces were concerned — the only life lost in the fort being that of a pet tom cat — yet it was not because our men were not exposed to death, or fighting for hours with his terrible shafts flying all around them. An omnipotent arm above shielded them from harm.

During a recent visit to the fort we acquainted ourselves with a number of interesting facts regarding the battle, a few of which we will give to the reader.

It will be recollected that the engagement took place on Tuesday, the 3d of March, instant. Including the attack on the Nashville, in which the fort became involved, it was the seventh attempt of the enemy to carry the position. That the reader may better understand the position of affairs, we would state that Fort McAllister is situated on the right bank of the Ogeechee, and occupies the farthest point of mainland jutting out into the marsh. The river flows straight from a point about a mile above the fort to a distance of about a mile and a half below, where it makes a bend and runs almost south and behind a point of wood, thence onward to Ossabaw sound and the ocean. During the afternoon of Monday, three iron monitors — the Montauk, the second supposed from the descriptions in the New York papers to be the Passaic, and the third the Weehawken [1] — steamed up from behind the point of wood, rounded the bend, and came up to within a short distance of the fort; the Montauk [2] about a thousand yards off, and the other two in the rear, some hundred and fifty yards from each other. Here they anchored in line of battle for the next day, and the night was passed in quiet, both sides no doubt busy with preparations for the dreadful work of the morrow. Around the

---

[1] The iron-clads designated were the Passaic, the Patapsco and the Nahant.

[2] Should be the Passaic.

point and a little over two miles distant, lay three mortar schooners and an old steamer, which also took part in the fight and kept up a rapid fire throughout. Such was the force and such the disposition of the enemy.

Our battery remained as in the former fight, except that it had been reinforced with a ten-inch Columbiad. Another part of our force on the day, which should not be overlooked, was a detachment of the Hardwick Mounted Rifles, Capt. McAllister, under command of Lieut. E. A. Elarbee. It consisted of Sergeant Hayman, and Privates Proctor, Wyatt, Harper and Cobb. These men went up the river and crossed over the marsh by night to a point about two hundred and fifty yards from the Montauk,[1] and in full rifle range, where they dug out a rifle pit in the mud and remained the greater part of the fight, it is believed not without important success, as will be seen hereafter.

Thus stood matters up to a quarter to nine o'clock Tuesday morning, when our troops, wearied with waiting on the enemy, opened on the Montauk [1] with the rifle gun. The eight-inch Columbiad, forty-two-pounder, and ten-inch Columbiad followed suit in the order in which they are named, all directing their fire on the Montauk.[1] At nine o'clock the Montauk [1] fired her first gun, and was followed by her associates in rapid succession. Thus commenced the firing on both sides, and the deadly strife was kept up steadily for seven and a half hours without the slightest intermission. Considering the strength of the combatants respectively, and the immense weight of metal thrown, in terrific grandeur there has been nothing like it since the commencement of the war; indeed, history furnishes no parallel. It is estimated that the enemy threw some two hundred and fifty shot and shell at the fort, amounting to some sixty or seventy tons of the most formidable missiles ever invented for the destruction of human life. Only think of eleven and fifteen-inch round shot, and rifle shells eight inches in diameter and seventeen inches in length, screaming along their

---

[1] Should be Passaic.

17

destructive way like so many fiery demons, plunging into the
earth-works of Fort McAllister to the depth of eight or ten
feet, or exploding with a voice of thunder and the jar of an
earthquake for more than seven mortal hours, over, around, and
in the midst of our undaunted little band of patriots! Firm
and unterrified they stood to their guns through it all, and at
the close, with a defiant shot and a shout of victory saluted the
retiring foe. Such a fire was never directed against mortal man
before, and they came out not only unscathed, but triumphant
from the fiery ordeal. About midday an eleven-inch shell struck
the upright post of the eight-inch Columbiad and shivered the
entire carriage to atoms; the gun was consequently lost to us
for the remainder of the day. The main traverse wheel of the
forty two-pounder was carried away by a shot, and replaced
within twenty minutes in the midst of a terrific fire. Private
Carroll Hanson, of the Emmett Rifles, distinguished himself by
passing out into the yard of the fort in the direct line of the
enemy's fire, where it appeared impossible for life to exist, and
returning by the same route with a wheel for the disabled gun.
One of the thirty-two's — which battery was gallantly served
throughout the fight by a detachment of sharp-shooters, under
command of Lieut. Herman — met with a similar accident, but
the fire was maintained during the entire engagement. These
guns were greatly exposed, and required the sternest kind of
nerves to man them.

About a quarter-past four o'clock, P. M., a shot from our forty-
two-pounder struck the body of the Montauk.[1] A volume of
steam was seen to issue from her side, and her turret refused to
revolve. She immediately weighed anchor, turned her bow
down stream, and retired from the fight. The fort gave her a
parting salute as she rounded, to which she replied by two
random shots, one of which went up the river and the other
across the marsh — as much as to say to her troublesome cus-
tomer: If I can't whip you, go to the d—l. The fort fired the first
and the last shot. In a few minutes the other two rams turned

---

[1] Should be Passaic.

about and followed their file leader, which, on making the bend below was taken in tow by a steamer, as if in a damaged condition.

Thus ended the fight, with the exception of a slow but continued fire, which was kept up from the mortar boats from behind the point of woods throughout the night, in order to prevent repairs on the fort. It, however, did little or no damage, nor did it cause a suspension of the work for a moment. The garrison being pretty well worn out by the labors of the day, Major Schaaff's battalion of sharp-shooters volunteered to make the necessary repairs. Though under fire, these brave men continued their work throughout the night, and at day-light the dismounted Columbiad was again in position, all the breaches repaired, and the fort in complete order for another trial of strength with her formidable antagonists. At dawn the men were again at their guns, but hour after hour passed and no enemy hove in sight. The Yankees had received their fill and concluded to let us alone.

But to revert to Lieut. Elarbee and his adventurous little band, who had taken their position under cover of the marsh within rifle shot of the enemy's rams. It was one of extreme peril, being not only exposed to a raking fire from the gun-boats, should they be discovered; but also in a direct line with the fire from the fort. During the fight, an officer made his appearance on the deck of the Montauk [1] with glass in hand, and presented the long wished for target. A Maynard rifle slug soon went whizzing by his ears, which startled and caused him to right about, when a second slug apparently took effect on his person, as with both hands raised he caught hold of the turret for support, and immediately clambered or was dragged in at a porthole. It is believed that the officer was killed. The display on the Montauk [1] the day following, and the funeral on Ossabaw, Friday, gave strength to the opinion.

As soon as this shot was fired, the Montauk [1] turned her guns upon the marsh and literally raked it with grape shot. The

---

[1] Should be Passaic.

riflemen, however, succeeded in changing their base in time to avoid the missiles of the enemy. Not one of them was hurt. Too much credit cannot be bestowed on this daring act of a few brave men.

Of the damage done to the garrison we have already given a full account, and can only repeat that it was confined to the wounding of one man — Thomas W. Rape, Emmett Rifles — in the knee, and another — William S. Owens, of the same company — slightly in the face. James Mims, of Co. D, 1st Georgia Battalion of Sharp-shooters, had his leg broken and his ankle crushed by the fall of a piece of timber while remounting the Columbiad after the fight. All, we learn, are doing well. Considerable havoc was made in the sand banks in the fort, and the quarters of the men were almost entirely demolished. The officers' quarters received two or three shots, but suffered no material damage. Inside the fort, and to the rear and left of it for half a mile, the earth was dug up into immense pits and furrows by the enemy's shell and shot — a large quantity of which has been gathered up and will be returned to the Yankees in a different form should the occasion offer.

It is almost incredible that our troops should have remained under such a fire for so long a time, and not one of them have been killed or seriously wounded. Indeed, their safety would seem to throw suspicion on the whole account of the fight. But it is all true, and why it is so cannot be accounted for on any principle of natural law. The escape was miraculous, and can only be ascribed to that All Seeing Eye that watches over the actions of men, and that Omnipotent Arm which is ever stretched out to uphold the right and shield from harm the cause of the just and oppressed. We might name a number of extraordinary incidents which occurred during the progress of the bombardment that baffle human reason and irresistibly turn the eye of the inquirer up to Him with whom all things are possible. A few will suffice :

The eleven-inch shell which shivered the carriage of the eight-inch Columbiad to atoms, exploded in the gun chamber in the midst of eight or ten men, and not one of them was injured.

A fragment the size of a man's head passed between Lieut. Dixon and number 1, of the gun detachment, who were within twenty inches of each other, and sank deep into the traverse without doing a particle of harm.

A shell fell and exploded in the pit of the rifle gun, where a number were serving, and but a single fragment was left on the floor, yet no one was hurt.

Several officers were lying in the door of the hospital, and four or five others standing around outside and not ten feet distant, when a fifteen-inch shell struck the bank, rolled down to the very door-sill and exploded. All were burnt with the powder, but not one was touched by the fragments of iron. Where they went to — who can tell?

This imperfect narrative has already attained to an unreasonable length, but it would hardly be just to close it without some special notice of the gallant spirits who were engaged in the fight. Where all acted so bravely and so well it would be wrong to discriminate, and we shall simply give the positions of the leading actors, that their names may become a part of the record.

Capt. Anderson of the Blues, as on a former trying occasion, was in command of the work, managed everything with good judgment and perfect coolness, and moved about from point to point wherever duty called him, without the first indication of fear. Capt. Nicoll of the Emmett Rifles, was present throughout the fight, and shrank from no post where his services were needed. We should not forget, too, the indefatigable Capt. McAllister of the Mounted Rifles, who has charge of the picket force of the coast, and whose watchful eye is hardly ever off the foe, day or night, and on whose information and advice most of our movements in that quarter are directed. He is ever on hand in a fight, and never fails to render essential service to the garrison. His men acted as couriers in the late fight, and were compelled to pass down the line of the enemy's fire whenever they entered the fort; but not one was known to flinch from his perilous duty.

Of the guns already alluded to, the eight-inch Columbiad — which somehow is a favorite mark of the enemy — was commanded, as before, by the fearless Lieut. Dixon, assisted by Sergeant Flood, who, by the way, was quite sick in the hospital, but left his bed to take part in the fight.

The rifle gun was commanded by Corporal Robert Smith of the Blues, assisted by a squad from that company.

The forty-two-pounder was in charge of Lieut. Quinn of the Blues, Sergeant Frazier assisting.

The ten-inch Columbiad fell to the lot of Lieut. Rockwell of the Emmett rifles, and was served with great efficiency by Sergeant Cavanagh and his squad.

The gallant Lieut. Willis, who distinguished himself by his skill and bravery in a former fight, was, to the regret of all, confined to his bed and unable to take part in the engagement.

The mortar battery, as in former engagements, was effectively served by Capt. Martin, with a detachment of his light artillerymen. They kept up a regular fire and threw their shells with a precision that would have done credit to veteran gunners.

All these gallant men stood firmly by their guns throughout the terrible conflict. Though often enveloped in smoke, and choked with clouds of flying sand, they fought to the last like heroes, and under the discouraging reflection that the cowardly foe, unlike themselves, were encased in impenetrable steel and secure from harm. Yet, a great work was before them—the iron-clad ships of the enemy were on trial, a test that was destined to affect most seriously the fortunes of the war—and they went to their work and stuck to it with as much resolution as if ten thousand of the foe were arrayed in open field before them. They whipped the fight, and taught the world a lesson in war which was unknown to it before, and indeed regarded as impossible. Let every Confederate soldier take courage from the glorious achievements of the noble Georgians at Genesis point. The last forlorn hope of the enemy has been driven back, leaving him to invent new plans to overcome and subdue the south.

Of Fort McAllister, itself, and its builders, we should say a word before closing. It is a monument to the professional skill and personal energy of Capt. McCrady, the engineer-in-chief of the district ; and to him and his no less energetic assistant, Capt. James McAlpin, the executor of the plan, is due a large share of the honors won on that day.

This brilliant victory drew from the brigadier general commanding the military district of Georgia, the following congratulatory order :

HEAD QUARTERS, DISTRICT GA.,
Savannah, March 3, 1863.

GENERAL ORDERS, No. 21.

In calling the attention of the troops in this district to the successful repulse on the 3d inst. of three turreted iron-clad gun-boats and three mortar boats by Fort McAllister, the brigadier general commanding again returns his hearty thanks to the brave garrison, and expresses the confident hope that their heroic example will be followed by all under his command. For eight hours these formidable vessels, throwing fifteen-inch hollow shot and shell, thirteen-inch shell, eleven-inch solid shot, and eight-inch rifle projectiles — a combination of formidable missiles never before concentrated upon a single battery — hurled an iron hail upon the fort ; but the brave gunners, with the cool efficient spirit of disciplined soldiers, and with the intrepid hearts of freemen battling in a just cause, stood undaunted at their posts, and proved to the world that the most formidable vessels and guns that modern ingenuity has been able to produce, are powerless against an earth-work, manned by patriots to whom honor and liberty are dearer than life. Believing that the repulse of these vessels, with but slight injury to the battery or garrison, marks a new era in the history of the war, the fact is published with proud satisfaction for the information and encouragement of all.

Captain Robert Martin, of Martin's Light Battery, who commanded the mortar during the engagement, and dropped one of his shells directly upon the deck of the Montauk,[1] deserves,

----

[1] Should be Passaic.

with his detachment, to share all the praise awarded to the immediate garrison.

The vigilance and activity of Capt. J. L. McAllister, and his free exposure to all danger, merit particular mention. His brave marksmen, who lay in the open marsh within rifle range of the gun-boats, are commended to the notice of the troops in this district.

The brigadier general commanding desires also to commend especially the gallant conduct of the First Battalion Georgia Sharp-shooters, officers and men. This corps, honorably distinguished for its discipline and drill, manned one of the guns of the battery throughout the fight; and during the ensuing night, under a severe and constant fire from the mortar boats, fearlessly repaired all the damage done to the fort, and rendered it by morning better prepared than ever to resist the foe.

The surgeons who volunteered their services and were present during the fight, the chief engineer, Capt. John McCrady, and his Assistant, James W. McAlpin, to whose zeal and efficient labors the repeated repulses of the abolition vessels are largely due, deserve honorable mention.

As a testimonial to the brave garrison, the commanding general will be solicited to direct that " Fort McAllister, March 3d, 1863," be inscribed upon their flags.

By command Brigadier General Mercer.

GEO. A. MERCER, A. A. G.

The general commanding the department of South Carolina, Georgia and Florida, in the following general orders complimented the brave defenders of Fort McAllister, and commended their courage and skill to the emulation of their brothers in arms :

HEAD QUARTERS, DEPT. of S. C., GA. and FLA.,
Charleston, S. C., March 18th, 1863.

GENERAL ORDERS, No. 42.

The commanding general has again a pleasant duty to discharge—to commend to the notice of the country, and the emulation of his officers and men the intrepid conduct of the garrison of Fort McAllister, and the skill of the officers engaged on the 3d of March, 1863.

Three iron-mailed vessels of the monitor species, armed with the heaviest ordnance used in modern warfare, and furnished with every appliance that an ingenious mechanical people could invent, for more than seven hours, assisted by two mortar schooners, concentrated an uninterrupted storm of shot and shell upon the brave inflexible men of Fort McAllister, whose coolness has added even to the credit won by officers and men on the previous attack by the enemy.

The colors of all troops engaged will be inscribed with, "Fort McAllister, 3d March, 1863."

By command of Gen. Beauregard.

THOMAS JORDAN,

Chief of Staff.

Never again during the continuance of the Confederate struggle for independence did the enemy venture upon another naval attack upon this battery. So far as the vaunted iron-clads and mortar boats and gun-boats were concerned, it proved itself an overmatch for all that had been sent against it. Upon seven different occasions were the Federals, in all their pride and pomp, repulsed before its bermuda-covered parapets; and it lived on, the pride of the district, the guardian of valuable interests upon the fertile banks of the beautiful Ogeechee, and the conspicuous witness of the valor of Georgia troops armed in the holy cause of truth, justice and national honor.

In December, 1864, when the Confederate flag, which had for more than three years floated so proudly from its ramparts, went down amid the smoke and the carnage of the assault of Gen. Hazen's division, Fort McAllister was not surrendered. It was overrun and captured by overwhelming numbes, the shock of

18

whose onset the combined and heroic efforts of its feeble and isolated garrison were powerless to withstand.

Subsequent to the engagement of the 3d of March the fort was most materially strengthened, especially in its rear defenses. Upon its improvement the best engineering skill of the district was bestowed. Its armament was essentially increased, so that late in the fall of 1864 its battery consisted of one ten-inch mortar, three ten-inch Columbiads, one eight-inch Columbiad, one forty-two-pounder gun, one thirty-two-pounder gun, rifled, four thirty-two-pounder guns, smooth-bore, one twenty-four-pounder howitzer, two twelve-pounder mountain howitzers, two twelve-pounder Napoleon guns, and six six-pounder bronze field guns, with a competent supply of ammunition.

The mission of this work was the defense of the Great Ogeechee river, and to that end its guns had been posted, and its general arrangements made. It was never intended to resist a serious or protracted land attack, although the field guns were designed to operate against surprise parties who might attempt to carry the fort by assault.

By the morning of the 11th of December, 1864, the Federal army under the command of Maj. Gen. Sherman, consisting of some sixty thousand infantry, fifty-five hundred cavalry and a full proportion of artillery, fat with the spoliations of Georgia, had completely enveloped the western lines erected for the defense of the city of Savannah extending from the Savannah river at Williamson's plantation, to the bridge of the Atlantic and Gulf rail road across the little Ogeechee. Such was the strength of the Confederate line, and so judiciously was it located, that the enemy feared the experiment of an assault, and sought an outlet to the sea and communication with an expectant fleet by an avenue other than the Savannah river. In consequence of the withdrawal of the small infantry force which for several days had been contesting the advance of the enemy on the right bank of the Great Ogeechee river, and by the retreat of the Confederate cavalry in the direction of Liberty county, Fort McAllister was left in an absolutely isolated position, and without the least possible chance of support or relief from any quarter.[1] Even after the most complete concentration of all the available Confederate forces upon the western defenses around Savannah, the morning report failed to show ten thousand men for duty in the trenches. Along that extended line there was in fact but a bare skirmish line, strengthened at important intervals.

It being absolutely necessary to the existence of the Federal army that communication with the coast should be established by the shortest route, and in the speediest manner, and it being deemed the part of prudence not to attempt to remove the lion in the

---

[1] In anticipation of the early isolation of the fort, and in view of the fact that neither relief for nor practical communication with that post could be had so soon as Gen. Sherman's army fully enveloped the western lines of Savannah, on the morning of the 8th of December 1,000 pounds of bacon, 2,250 pounds of hard bread, and other rations in proportion — amounting in all to thirty-two days' rations for 200 men — were issued from Savannah and safely conveyed to the fort. Extra supplies, consisting of 40 gallons of whiskey, 40 gallons of molasses, 50 pounds of candles, and some soap and salt were issued and received at the same time.

On the 9th, fifteen days' rations were added to the above, so that the fort was amply provided for any period during which it was possible for our forces to maintain its possession. Fort McAllister was doomed the very moment Sherman's army appeared before the city of Savannah, and the capture of its small garrison depended entirely upon the will of the enemy.

path, it was resolved to carry Fort McAllister, and thus open up the Great Ogeechee to the fleet which had so often and in vain essayed its ascent.

Accordingly the second division of the fifteenth corps under command of Brig. Gen. Hazen, consisting of nine regiments, was, on the morning of the 13th of December put in motion for the accomplishment of this important object. Crossing the Great Ogeechee at King's bridge, this force arrived in the vicinity of the fort about one o'clock in the afternoon.

For the following account of the assault and capture of Fort McAllister I am indebted to Major George W. Anderson, then commanding, whose name is intimately and honorably connected with the defense of this heroic earth-work:

Hearing incidentally that the Confederate forces on the Cannouchee had evacuated that position and retired across the Great Ogeechee, and learning that a large column of the enemy was approaching in the direction of Fort McAllister, I immediately detached a scouting party under command of Second Lieutenant T. O'Neal, of Clinch's Light Battery, to watch them and acquaint me with their movements. This was absolutely necessary, as the cavalry previously stationed in Bryan county had been withdrawn, and I was thus thrown upon my own resources for all information relating to the strength and designs of the enemy. On the morning of the 12th of December, 1864, I accompanied Lieutenant O'Neal on a scout, and found the enemy advancing in force from King's bridge. We were hotly pursued by their cavalry, and had barely time to burn the barns of Messrs. Thomas C. Arnold and William Patterson, which were filled with rice. The steam-tug Columbus — lying about three miles above the fort — was also burned. Early the next morning one of my pickets—stationed at the head of the causeway west of the fort — was captured by the enemy, to whom he imparted the fact that the causeway was studded with torpedoes, in time to prevent their explosion. He also acquainted them with the strength of the garrison, and the armament of the fort, and the best approaches to it.

About eight o'clock, A. M., desultory firing commenced between the skirmishers of the enemy and my sharp-shooters. At ten o'clock the fight became general, the opposing forces extending from the river entirely around to the marsh on the east. The day before, the enemy had established a battery of Parrott guns on the opposite side of the river — distant from the fort a mile and a half — which fired upon us at regular intervals during that day and the ensuing night.[1] Receiving from head quarters neither orders nor responses to my telegraphic dispatches, I determined under the circumstances, and notwithstanding the great disparity of numbers between the garrison and the attacking forces, to defend the fort to the last extremity. The guns being *en barbette*, the detachments serving them were greatly exposed to the fire of the enemy's sharp-shooters. To such an extent was this the case, that in one instance, out of a detachment of eight men, three were killed and three more wounded. The Federal skirmish line was very heavy, and the fire so close and rapid that it was at times impossible to work our guns. My sharp-shooters did all in their power, but were entirely too few to suppress this galling fire upon the artillerists. In view of the large force of the enemy — consisting of nine regiments, whose aggregate strength was estimated between 3,500 and 4,000 muskets, and possessing the ability to increase it at any time should it become necessary — and recollecting the feebleness of the garrison of the fort, numbering only 150 effective men, it was evident, cut off from all support, and with no possible hope of reenforcements from any quarter, that holding the fort was simply a question of time. There was but one alternative, death or captivity. Captain Thomas S. White, the engineer in charge, had previously felled the trees in the vicinity of the

---

[1] The light artillery here alluded to consisted of a section of De Grase's Battery, posted near the rice mill on Dr. Cheves's plantation.

fort, and demolished the mortar magazine which commanded the fort to a very considerable extent. For lack of the necessary force and time, however, the felled timber and the ruins of the adjacent houses which had been pulled down, had not been entirely removed. Protected by this cover, the enemy's sharpshooters were enabled to approach quite near, to the great annoyance and injury of the cannoneers. One line of abattis had been constructed by the engineer, and three lines would have been completed around the fort, but for the want of time and material.

Late in the afternoon the full force of the enemy made a rapid and vigorous charge upon the works, and, succeeding in forcing their way through the abattis, rushed over the parapet of the fort, carrying it by storm, and, by virtue of superior numbers, overpowered the garrison, fighting gallantly to the last. In many instances the Confederates were disarmed by main force. *The fort was never surrendered. It was captured by overwhelming numbers.* So soon as the enemy opened fire upon the fort from the opposite side of the river, it was evident that two of the magazines were seriously endangered, and it became necessary to protect them from that fire by the erection of suitable traverses. The labor expended in their construction, in the mounting of guns on the rear of the work, and in removing the debris above referred to, occupied the garrison constantly night and day for nearly forty-eight hours immediately preceding the attack. Consequently, at the time of the assault, the men were greatly fatigued and in bad plight, physically considered, for the contest. I think it not improper to state here, that a short time before the approach of the enemy a member of the torpedo department, had, in obedience to orders, placed in front of the fort, and along the direct approaches, a considerable number of sub-terra shells, whose explosions killed quite a number of the enemy while passing over them.

After the capture of the fort, General Sherman in person ordered my engineer, with a detail of sixteen men from the garrison — then prisoners of war — to remove all the torpedoes which had not exploded. This hazardous duty was performed without injury to any one; but it appearing to me to be an unwarrantable and improper treatment of prisoners of war, I have thought it right to refer to it in this report.

I am pleased to state that in my endeavors to hold the fort, I was nobly seconded by the great majority of officers and men under my command. Many of them had never been under fire before, and quite a number were very young, in fact mere boys. Where so many acted gallantly, it would be invidious to discriminate; but I cannot avoid mentioning those who came more particularly under my notice. I would therefore most respectfully call the attention of the general commanding to the gallant conduct of Captain Clinch, who, when summoned to surrender by a Federal captain, responded by dealing him a severe blow on the head with his sabre. (Captain Clinch had previously received two gun-shot wounds in the arm). Immediately a hand to hand fight ensued. Federal privates came to the assistance of their officer, but the fearless Clinch continued the unequal contest until he fell bleeding from eleven wounds (three sabre wounds, six bayonet wounds, and two gun-shot wounds), from which, after severe and protracted suffering, he has barely recovered. His conduct was so conspicuous, and his cool bravery so much admired, as to elicit the praise of the enemy and even of General Sherman himself.

First Lieutenant William Schirm fought his guns until the enemy had entered the fort, and, notwithstanding a wound in the head, gallantly remained at his post, discharging his duties with a coolness and efficiency worthy of all commendation.

Lieutenant O'Neal whom I placed in command of the scouting party before mentioned, while in the discharge of that duty, and in his subsequent conduct during the attack, merited the honor due to a faithful and gallant officer.

Among those who nobly fell, was the gallant Hazzard, whose zeal and activity were worthy of all praise. He died as a true soldier at his post facing overwhelming odds.

The garrison consisted of

The Emmett Rifles, Captain George A. Nicoll, commanding, numbering for duty, 25 men.

Clinch's Light Battery, Captain N. B. Clinch commanding, numbering for duty, 50 men.

Company D, 1st Regiment Georgia Reserves, Captain Henry commanding, numbering for duty, 28 men.

Company E, 1st Regiment Georgia Reserves, Captain Morrison commanding, numbering for duty, 47 men.

Total, 150 men.

Casualties.

Commissioned — Captain N. B. Clinch.   Eleven wounds.

Captain Morrison.   Shot through both legs.

First Lieut. Schirm.   Shot in the head.

Killed, Second Lieut. Hazzard.

Privates and non-commissioned — Killed, 16 ; wounded, 28.

Total killed and wounded, 48.

When the stifling dust and ashes came thick and fast from the volcano and the liquid lava streamed down, and the frightened populace fled in wild dismay, the sentinel at the gate of Pompeii stood unflinchingly at his post.   We are told that his bones in their helmet and breast-plate, with the hand still raised to keep the suffocating dust from the mouth and nose, remain even until our times to show how a Roman soldier did his duty.   It is recorded that in like manner the last of the old Spanish infantry, originally formed by the great Capt. Gonzalo de Cordova, were all cut off, standing fast to a man at the battle of Rocroy.   The whole regiment was found lying in regular order upon the field of battle, with their colonel, the old Count de Fuentes at their head, expiring in a chair in which he had been carried, because he was too infirm to walk, to this, his twentieth battle.   Well might the conqueror, the high-spirited young Duke D'Enghien, exclaim in view of such valor, " Were I not a victor, I should have wished thus to die."

The heroism of the past has been fully equalled in the self-devotion and the manliness of the present; and when the golden deeds wrought by Confederates in the holy cause of liberty and of right shall be garnered up in sacred remembrance, the recollection of Fort McAllister and its brave defenders will be perpetuated in all honor, and cherished with peculiar pride by every true hearted Georgian.

The enemy admit a loss of ninety men in this assault upon the fort. With its fall facile communication was established between Gen. Sherman's army and the Federal fleet. One week afterwards the city of Savannah was successfully evacuated, and the Confederate forces, in the immediate presence of an enemy outnumbering them more than eight to one, crossing the river upon pontoons, and moving, within but a few hundred yards of large Federal detachments, along the rice dams, reached the high grounds of South Carolina in safety. Every piece of light Artillery capable of being moved was brought off, and all the transportation of the army saved. Viewed in the light of surrounding circumstances, this retreat, properly considered, should be regarded as a Confederate triumph. On the morning of the night of the evacuation, the field report showed an aggregate present for duty in the city of Savannah, along the western lines, and in the fixed batteries, of only 9,089 men. This aggregate included Confederate troops of all arms of the service, state troops, reserves, militia, and home guards.

About the middle of February, 1863, the two sections of the Chatham Artillery which, during the recent attacks upon Fort McAllister had been posted, one of the m within supporting distance of the fort, and the other higher up the Great Ogeechee and in

19

the neighborhood of King's bridge, were ordered back
to Camp Ashby at White Bluff.

On the 19th of May, this company and the Terrell
Artillery — Capt. J. W. Brooks — were temporarily
formed into a battalion under the command of Maj.
E. G. Dawson. This organization was, however, perpetuated only until the sixteenth of June, when Maj.
Dawson tendered his resignation on account of ill
health, and the company resumed its status as an
independent battery.

The next day the first permanent and valuable
change in the armament of the Battery was made in
pursuance of the following orders :

HEAD QUARTERS, LIGHT ARTILLERY,
Savannah, Ga., June 16th, 1863.

SPECIAL ORDERS, No. 56.

I. Captain Wheaton commanding Chatham Artillery, will, at
at an early hour to-morrow morning, send in to these head quarters the six-pounder section of his battery, with ammunition,
implements, limbers, caissons and everything pertaining to it,
under charge of a commissioned officer, with suitable detachments.

II. That section, with the exception of the harness belonging to it, will be turned over to the ordnance officer ; and in its
stead a complete section of twelve-pounder guns of the Napoleon
pattern will be placed in the possession of the company.

It is with sincere pleasure that the lieutenant colonel commanding finds himself able to furnish this battery — which by
its proficiency has attracted to itself the favorable notice, not
only of the district but also of the department commander —
with a section of guns so complete in appointment, and capable
of rendering such efficient service in the field.

He confidently trusts and believes that the reputation earned
for itself by this battery will be honestly sustained, alike amid

the tiresome routine of camp duties, and, whenever the occasion presents itself, amid the dangers of the battle-field.

*   *   *   *   *   *   *   *   *   *

By command of

CHARLES C. JONES, JR.,

Lieut. Colonel Commanding.

George A. Whitehead,

Adjutant.

Some months before, the other section of six-pounder guns had been exchanged for a section of twelve-pounder howitzers; and, for a short period during the month of March, 1863, the company had charge of a section of three and one-half-inch Blakely rifle guns. These, however, were soon returned to the ordnance officer, there having been some mistake in their issue.

During the remaining period of the encampment of the company at Camp Ashby, but little occurred to vary the monotony of the customary drills, target practice, and daily duties. The storm of battle which visited with its desolating influences many other portions of the Confederacy, did not descend upon these immediate borders, and for the time being all was comparative peace.

The death of that great Christian warrior, the genius of the war — Lieut. Gen. Thomas J. Jackson — had, in obedience to the following general orders, been commemorated with feelings of the most profound sorrow within the department:

HEAD QUARTERS, DEPT. S. C., GA., and FLA.,

Charleston, May 13, 1863.

GENERAL ORDERS, No. 67.

The illustrious soldier, Lieut. Gen. Thomas J. Jackson is dead. The memory of his high worth, conspicuous virtues, and momentous services will be treasured in the heart, and incite the pride of country to all time.   His renown is already identified with our revolution, and even our enemy admits his unselfish devotion to our cause, and admires his eminent qualities.

The commanding generals of the 1st military district, and of the district of Georgia, on the day following the reception of this order, will cause a gun to be fired at every half hour, beginning at sunrise and ending at sunset ; and the flags at every post in the department will be hoisted at half mast in token of the national bereavement.

By command of

GENERAL BEAUREGARD.

Thomas Jordan, Chief of Staff.

CHAPTER VI.

Battery ordered to James island. Affair of the 16th of July, with the
    Pawnee. Operations on Morris island resulting in the reduction of
    Batteries Wagner and Gregg, and the silencing of the barbette fire
    of Fort Sumter.

The movements of the Federals upon the coast of
South Carolina indicating very plainly the inaugura-
tion of a new and serious effort to possess themselves
of the outposts, and ultimately of the city of Charleston itself, a concentration of troops was ordered by
Gen. Beauregard for the protection of the approaches
to that city, and the stronger occupation of its harbor
defenses.   The Chatham Artillery, in obedience to
orders received late in the afternoon of that day, on
the night of the 9th of July, 1863, marched from Camp
Ashby at White Bluff to Savannah, and thence proceeded the next day by the Charleston and Savannah
rail road to Charleston, arriving in that city about ten
o'clock P. M.   Upon reporting at head quarters of the
department for further orders, the Battery was directed
to proceed with all haste the same night to James
island, and report for duty to Col. Simonton commanding the advanced lines.   The march — although
along strange roads, sadly out of repair and during
a very dark night — was accomplished without accident.   At day-break on the morning of the 11th the
battery reported at Secessionville to Col. Simonton,
ready for immediate duty and in perfect order.   At
this time the enemy was present in considerable force

on the lower end of James island, and a formidable advance was daily expected. For four consecutive nights after its arrival the Battery was kept in position on the advanced lines — horses harnessed and hitched to the pieces, and detachments at their posts — in momentary anticipation of an attack.

The Federals failing to advance, it was deemed best to make an effort to drive them from the island. Accordingly, all the available Confederate forces were put in motion early on the morning of the 16th. The effect of this demonstration was seen in the hasty withdrawal of the enemy, and their abandonment of the effort to secure a lodgment upon James island.

The part borne by the Chatham Artillery in this affair of the 16th, is truthfully detailed in the following letter written a few days after, by Captain Wheaton, who was present, directing the movements of his command with that energy, ability and patriotism, which, during the long and tedious hours of this protracted struggle, characterized him as an officer :

HEAD QUARTERS, CHATHAM ARTILLERY,
Advanced Lines, James Island, July 20th, 1863.
Colonel Charles C. Jones, Jr.,
    Savannah, Geo.

Colonel : Your note of the 14th inst. did not reach me until yesterday. I had forwarded my ordnance returns for the last quarter, previous to its receipt. The telegraph keeps you so fully informed of what transpires here, that any news which I might give of a general character would be old before it reached you. I will therefore confine myself to the part taken by my company in the engagement of the 16th inst. At ten o'clock on the night of the 15th, I received orders to have my section of howitzers, fully equipped, each piece and caisson supplied with eight horses, at Secessionville, by 12 P. M., there to await further orders from Col. Way. While placing that section in marching order, a second courier arrived with instructions for me to prepare my Napoleon section for action, and to report with it at a certain cross roads to Col. Ratcliff of the 61st North Carolina. Both sections reported promptly, according to their respective orders. Arriving with the Napoleon section at the point designated, Col. Ratcliff informed me that he had been ordered with his own regiment, my section, a Napoleon section of Capt. Blake's South Carolina battery, and a siege train, to proceed to Grimball's point on the Stono river and there attack the United States gun-boat Pawnee, and another gun-boat, the name of which was then unknown, both lying in the river abreast the position designated. Capt. Blake's section reported promptly. We awaited patiently for three hours the arrival of the siege train, but it failed to make its appearance. Col. Ratcliff then, with the advice of Lieut. Col. Del Kemper, who had intermediately reported for duty, decided to move forward with the force under his command, as it was all important that we should reach the point specified before daylight. We accordingly took up the line of march and reached our pickets just as the first indications of approaching day were visible in the east. Our picket lines rested in the edge of a thick wood, which they skirted for a distance of a mile and a half. Beyond, were old fields a quarter of a mile in width, which had to be crossed in full view of the gun-boats of the enemy before we could reach the position assigned to us for offensive operations. The necessary arrangements having been made, the infantry deployed to the right and left of the road, and soon came up with and drove in the Federal pickets. As soon as the infantry had deployed and were moving well to the front, we started at a round trot, which was very shortly afterwards increased to a gallop, and came into battery in handsome style within five hundred yards of the gun-boats. Both sections, my own and Capt. Blake's, opened fire simultanously, and with a will. Crash, went shot after, shot into the monster sides of the vessels, nearly every shot taking effect.

After having fired some ten rounds, we observed great confusion on board both vessels, which soon opened upon us with their heavy guns. A moment afterwards two other gun-boats, about a mile lower down the river, also opened upon us. Nothing dismayed, we continued our firing with great spirit. Both of the advanced vessels slipped their cables and commenced moving down the river, making all haste to get out of the range of our guns. We continued firing from our first position for some minutes longer, when we limbered to the front, and advancing at a gallop to the bank of the river, again opened fire with shells which exploded beautifully right over and on the Pawnee's deck. At one time her pilot house was set on fire. Screaming and great confusion on board could be distinctly heard and seen by our advanced pickets who enjoyed a fine view of the engagement.

She soon, however, got beyond the range of our guns, and it being impracticable, on account of the soft and marshy character of the river bank, for us to pursue her farther, we limbered up and took a position to the left of our first position, expecting an attack from the land forces of the enemy. They were, however, so actively engaged by our troops on the left, that they had no opportunity to pay any attention to us. Not so the gun-boats however. They rained upon us a perfect torrent of shells which fell in front, and rear, and all around us, sometimes falling and exploding so near as to cover the men with dirt, and yet, strange to say, wounding neither man nor horse of either battery. Our infantry support lost one man killed. One was seriously, and several were slightly wounded.

After remaining for about an hour under this fire we received orders to retire, the gun-boats continuing their shelling until we reached our camp.

An incident occurred while we were changing our position from the one first taken to that nearer the river bank, which will give you an idea of the spirit with which my men went into the fight, and of their conduct under fire. As we were advancing at a round gallop (a very thick growth of weeds completely obscuring the ground), my right piece ran into a pit at least six feet deep, leaders first, then the centre team, then the wheel-horses, and finally the limber, piled on the top of all.

No one could view the situation and think it possible that either horses or drivers could escape without serious injury. The piece had to be unlimbered before they could be extricated, and they lay in such a position that this could not be done until the right wheel of the limber was raised to a level. I saw the situation at a glance, and ordered the prolonge to be uncoiled and made fast to the lower part of the wheel, and then passed over the limber. The men executed the order so systematically and promptly, that in less than five minutes we had limber, horses and drivers all out, without having sustained any serious injury. Even the harness encountered no material damage. During the time that we were thus employed, shells were exploding all around us, but my men paid no more attention to them than they would have done to so many puff balls.

Our Napoleon section fired one hundred and four rounds during the engagement. The expenditure of ammunition by Capt. Blake's section was about the same. A great number of our shots took effect, but we did not accomplish what we hoped, to wit, the capture of at least one of the vessels. That they were seriously endamaged by our fire, there can be no doubt. There is also every reason to believe that a goodly number of lives was lost on board, as the flags of the Federal vessels lower down the Stono were at half mast all day Friday.

The howitzer section did not fire a shot. As it was about to open upon the enemy, it was ordered to hold itself as a reserve; which order was reluctantly obeyed.

The object of the reconnoissance was announced as accomplished, and our forces were ordered to retire. Subsequent events conclusively demonstrated the fact that if we had vigorously prosecuted the attack, we would have captured the entire Federal force on the island. The enemy evacuated James island the same night; in their haste abandoning a considerable amount of stores. They are now supposed to be on one of the smaller islands below.

Since leaving home (Camp Ashby) we have been constantly on duty, last night being the first that our horses have passed with the harness off. My men have borne it well, when it is remembered that they have not thus far had a night's sleep, that it has rained every day since we have been on the island, that we are without tents, except a limited number for the sick, and consequently that we have been at all times entirely exposed to the influences of these hot suns and drenching showers. I have only ten on the sick list to-day, two of whom I have sent to the hospital in Charleston. We have excellent medical attendance, with a full supply of medicines, and requisite comforts for the sick.

Since writing the above, the enemy have commenced shelling Battery Wagner again. They have been terribly punished there.

 * * * * * * * *

I am, colonel, very respectfully,

Your obedient servant,

Jno. F. Wheaton.

P. S. I should have mentioned in the proper connection, that after Captain Blake's section and my own had engaged the enemy's gun-boats for about twenty minutes, the siege train arrived upon the ground and added its fire to that of the other pieces.

From the 10th of July, 1863, until the evacuation of the city of Charleston by the Confederate forces under Lieut. Gen. Wm. J. Hardee, the Chatham Artillery remained — with occasional exceptions which will hereafter be specifically noted — continuously on duty on James island, an eye-witness of, and a participant in those scenes of privation, of heroic endurance and of patient valor, which, when fully grouped, present one of the most impressive pictures in the history of this eventful war. With the defense of Wagner, with the memories of Secessionville, Fort Johnson, Grimball's point, and the advanced lines, the name and good deeds of this Battery are thoroughly identified. Ever ready to meet the enemy —

PLAN
OF THE
APPROACH AND ATTACK ON FORT SUMTER,
BY THE
FEDERAL IRON CLAD FLEET.
7 APRIL. 1863.
SCALE OF MILES.

DRAWN TO ACCOMPANY ENGINEER REPORT.

Wm. H. Echols,
Major &c.

Rope Obstructions

Fort Moultrie

S U L L I V A N S I

Baty Beauregard

Maffitts Channel

Fort Sumter

BUOY No. 3

Cummings Point

Vincents Creek

Baty Wagner

M O R R I S

W. A. Walker, C. S. Eng. Corps

Charleston 11 April 1863

bearing up with cheerful courage under the burning suns and malarial influences of summer, and the frosts and rains of winter—uncomplaining under the frequently inadequate issues of rations and clothing—unaffected by the depreciation of the Confederate currency which rendered the entire month's pay of a private soldier insufficient to procure one generous meal in a decent restaurant—whether in action, on picket duty, upon drill or parade, or in camp, the members of this Battery responded with such intelligence, alacrity, and efficiency to the discharge of every duty devolved upon them, that they secured and maintained for their company the enviable and well deserved reputation of being the finest light battery in the department.

A brief allusion to some of the more important events which transpired in the immediate presence of the Battery during its first term of service on James island may not prove entirely uninteresting, and will serve to awaken proud recollections of one of the grandest sieges in the annals of ancient or modern warfare.

The attack upon Fort Sumter by the Federal iron-clad fleet under Rear Admiral Dupont, on the 7th of April, 1863, signally failed. After an engagement which lasted scarcely three-quarters of an hour, the Keokuk was so much injured that she sunk abreast of Morris island, and the rest of the iron-clads retired baffled of their enterprise and considerably damaged.

Although in this engagement the barbette fire of the fort proved too powerful for these vaunted mailed monitors, the masonry walls suffered from the effects of this bombardment far more than was generally known. Although this fact was concealed from the enemy, the lessons which it brought home to the appreciation of the Confederate engineers proved of great benefit in the subsequent arrangements for the defense of the city of Charleston. Up to this time there had been a constant and formidable concentration of the best guns which could be procured, upon the parapet and in the casemates of Sumter.

The assault of Gen. Benham upon the advanced works upon James island in June of the previous year, had resulted in a bloody and most disastrous repulse.

Morris island was occupied by Confederate troops holding three fortified positions, viz: Battery Gregg, at the north end, Battery Wagner nearer the middle, and the batteries at the south end of the island designed to command the entrance into Light-house inlet, and to prevent a hostile landing from Folly island. The armament of these last mentioned batteries consisted of two eight-inch navy guns, one eight-inch navy shell gun, two eight-inch sea-coast howitzers, one three-inch Whitworth gun, three ten-inch sea-coast mortars, one thirty-pounder navy Parrott rifle and one Brooke rifle gun.

These pieces were so arranged in detached, and yet mutually supporting batteries, as not only to cover with their fire the north end of Folly island in the possession of the enemy, and the main ship channel abreast of Morris island, but also to sweep almost the entire length of Light-house inlet which separates these two islands.

Disheartened by their experiences in front of Sumter, and the James island lines, the enemy determined, in prosecuting their efforts to compass the reduction of Charleston, to vary their approaches; and accordingly fixed upon the capture of Morris island as the objective of their new operations.

About the middle of June, with a view to the accomplishment of this purpose, the Federals commenced the accumulation of ordnance and ordnance stores on the north end of Folly island. With such energy and secrecy were these operations conducted, that by the 6th of July they had, without interruption, and without the knowledge of the Confederates who were in force just across Light-house inlet, completed the construction of ten fixed batteries, masked, and mounting forty-seven guns.

In such utter ignorance were the Confederates of the precise character and extent of the Federal operations on the north point of Folly island, and of the number of troops concentrated in that vicinity, that an expedition was on foot almost the day before the formidable demonstration of the 9th of July, whose object was the capture of the small force supposed to be stationed there and occupying a camp of observation.

Shortly after day-break on the morning of the 9th of July the Federal batteries opened a concentrated, heavy, and well directed fire against our Light-house inlet batteries. Under cover of this fire, taking advantage of the effect produced by this powerful and unlooked for demonstration, Brig. Gen. Strong succeeded in crossing and landing his command, and in capturing successively the Confederate batteries on the south end of Morris island. Vigorously pushing his success, he advanced along the island until his progress was arrested by Battery Wagner.

At daylight on the morning of the 11th, Battery Wagner was assaulted by a brigade of the enemy under command of Brig. Gen. Strong. The fort was then commanded by Colonel Graham of the 21st South Carolina regiment, and its garrison consisted of a battalion of the First Regiment Georgia Volunteers, Col. Charles H. Olmstead, of the 12th Battalion Georgia Volunteers; Lt. Col. Capers, of the 18th Battalion Georgia Volunteers; Major Basinger, and several companies of South Carolina regulars. This attempt to carry the fort by storm was gallantly frustrated, and the enemy compelled to retreat in confusion, leaving ninety-five dead in front of the battery, and one hundred and thirty prisoners in our hands.

During the 18th, the fort sustained a terrific bombardment from four Federal batteries on Morris island, viz: Battery Reynolds, distant from Wagner 1,330 yards, and armed with five eight-inch siege mortars, two thirty-pounder and six ten-pounder Parrott rifles, four three-inch rifles and two Wiard guns; Battery Weed, distant 1,460 yards, and mounting four ten-inch siege mortars; Battery Hays, distant 1,830 yards, and mounting nine thirty-pounder and four twenty-pounder Parrott rifles; and Battery O'Rourke, 1,920 yards distant, and comprising five ten-inch siege mortars. The iron-clad fleet also closed in opposite the fort, and took a very active part in the engagement. To resist this tremendous array of formidable guns, Battery Wagner possessed an armament of two ten-inch Columbiads, two eight-inch navy shell guns, one ten-inch siege howitzer, two eight-inch siege howitzers, one ten-inch mortar, three thirty-two-pounder guns, three carronades and five field pieces.

During the earlier portions of the bombardment the fort responded freely from its heaviest guns, but when it became evident that no material injury could be inflicted upon the monitors, and that the Battery was powerless to cope successfully with the guns of the enemy, the fire of the fort slackened, and the garrison — except such sentinels as were needed on post —

was ordered within the bomb-proof, where it remained sheltered from the terrific storm of rifle shot shells and spherical case.

As the result of that awful bombardment, nearly sixteen feet of the sand covering of the bomb-proof were carried away. The outline of the parapets was seriously changed. But for the presence of that bomb-proof, the garrison must have perished. In the language of one of the officers on duty in the fort during that memorable day, a bird could not have lived five minutes beyond the immediate shelter of the bomb-proof and the parapet. The fort was converted by these exploding projectiles into a perfect volcano, casting up each moment clouds of fire, smoke and dust. Never before in the history of wars had such a tremendous fire been concentrated within and upon such a small work. To the eye of the observer the Battery appeared doomed to utter annihilation.

Late in the afternoon, the watchful eye of Brig. Gen. Taliaferro commanding, discovered indications of an early assault. Immediately the garrison left the bomb-proof and prepared to meet the onset. The enemy soon after advanced in heavy force. The attack was gallantly led and vigorously sustained. At one time the fort was well-nigh carried, but the heroic efforts of the garrison finally achieved a signal triumph, capturing those of the enemy who had effected a lodgment in one angle of the work, and compelling the rest of the assailants to seek safety in flight.

With this second repulse of the Federals in front of Wagner, dates an entire change in the military policy adopted by the enemy. No more attempts were made to carry that fort by storm. Thenceforward resort was had to slow and securely constructed approaches, severe and prolonged bombardments, and

continued sharp shooting, which finally compelled the
evacuation of that bravely defended post on the night
of the 6th of September.

So long as the muse of history delights to repeat
the story of the white cross of the order of St. John,
and with throbbing breast recounts the brave deeds of
the grand master and his hardy knights in defense of
the castle of St. Elmo; when of bold Horatius she tells

> How valiantly he kept the bridge
> In the brave days of old;

while men pause in mute admiration of the wonderful siege of Zaragoza, and the sublime courage of
Agostina; until the names of Leonidas and of Megis-
tias are blotted from the record of patriotic devotion,
let the memories of Wagner and of Sumter, and of
the noble hearted Confederates who defended them,
be cherished with equal honor and veneration.

Fort Wagner was simply an inclosed earth-work
occupying the entire breadth of Morris island (which
at that point is quite narrow), extending from high
water mark on the east, to Vincent's creek and impracticable marshes on the west. Its faces were
mutually defensive, and thoroughly flanked. Having
an excellent command, and a bold relief, it was further provided with a sluice gate for retaining the high
water in the ditch. Constructed of compact sand,
the damages caused by the heaviest projectiles could,
under ordinary circumstances, be rapidly repaired.
A tolerably capacious and well protected bomb-proof
afforded shelter for its garrison. The armament of
this work has already been given.

The shore batteries on James island, Fort Sumter,
and Battery Gregg—although at rather long ranges—
were within supporting distances of Wagner.

Perceiving the important part which Fort Sumter would bear in resisting the efforts for the reduction of Battery Wagner, and emboldened by the success which crowned their bombardment of Fort Pulaski from Tybee island, soon after the repulse of the 18th the enemy resolved upon the early elimination of Fort Sumter from the conflict. Accordingly their attention was at once directed to the construction of breaching batteries armed with the heaviest rifle guns, then unknown in modern warfare. With these Fort Sumter was to be reduced over the head of Wagner. At the same time parallels with flying saps were established against Wagner.[1]

In the prosecution of this purpose, the progress of the enemy was most seriously retarded, and at times almost wholly checked by the converging fire of Wagner, Gregg, Sumter, and the James island batteries, Fort Johnson, Simkins, Cheves, Haskell, Ryan and Ramsey, and especially by the sharp-shooters from Wagner, who were constantly on the alert.

Apprehending the design of the enemy, the most valuable guns were secretly, and as rapidly as possible, under cover of the night, removed from Fort Sumter; and every effort was made by the Confederates to strengthen its passive means of defense, by the use of sand bags and cotton bales. The shore batteries on James island were also materially strengthened, and supplied with every available gun which could be procured.

On account of the isolated position of Wagner and the precarious means of communication, but little

---

[1] See Major General Gillmore's report.

21

could be accomplished in its behalf. The night was consumed by the garrison in repairing the damages sustained during the day. So exhausting were the labors — so oppressive the atmosphere of the bomb-proof — and so severe the ordeal, that the garrison had to be changed at intervals of five days or a week. Human nature could not for a longer period sustain such privations, fatigues, and ceaseless dangers. Access to the fort could be had only under cover of the night, in small boats coming over from Fort Johnson on James island. The men were compelled to carry cooked rations with them, as there was no accumulation of supplies within the fort. Cooking could not be done within the bomb-proof, and, such was the severity of the enemy's fire, it could not be carried on without. As far as practicable fresh water in barrels was furnished the garrison, but the supply was meagre and precarious. The water obtained from the wells within the bomb-proof was brackish and fetid.[1]

Probably on no occasion within the history of this war — so replete with hardships, privations, and dangers — was a garrison called upon to endure so much. These were indeed times which tried men's souls, and it required the truest patriotism and the surest courage to sustain the Confederate soldier as he passed day by day through this fiery trial. Three times did the Chatham Artillery respond to the exigences of the hour, each time furnishing a detachment of thirty men, exclusive of the officer in charge.

The first detachment went over by boats from Fort Johnson on the night of the 29th of July, Lieut. Askew commanding.

---

[1] The shallow springs dug by the men, actually bred worms.

The second detachment reached Fort Wagner on the night of the 10th of August, by same conveyance, Lieut. Palmer commanding; and the third detachment went over to the fort on the night of the 26th of August, Lieut. Askew again in command. On the 28th, Lieut. Hendry joined this detachment while in Battery Wagner.

To the detachments from the light batteries on James island, serving in rotation at Wagner, were assigned the field pieces in position within that fort.

Thus, during the darkest days of that terrible siege did the Chatham Artillery share in the hardships, the dangers and the privations of the hour. To its members also belong equal rights in the honor of the defense. It was the remark of an officer fresh from the appalling scenes and perils which he had witnessed and endured for twelve long days within the walls of Wagner: "I wonder how the men endure the service at Wagner. The fire of the enemy is enough to demoralize an angel."

At day-break on the 17th of August the Federals opened fire upon Sumter from twelve breaching batteries, mounting in the aggregate forty-three guns, as follows:

One ten-inch Parrott rifle, three hundred-pounder; six eight-inch Parrott rifles, two hundred-pounders; nine one hundred-pounder Parrott rifles; ten thirty-pounder Parrott rifles; two eighty-pounder Whitworth rifles; twelve ten-inch mortars; three Coehorn mortars; and located at distances from the centre of the gorge wall of the fort varying from 3,516 to 4,290 yards. Breaching batteries of such power and range were never before concentrated in the history of wars. This bombardment while particularly directed at, was not wholly confined to Fort Sumter. It extended also

to Battery Wagner, Battery Gregg, and occasionally
to Shell Point Battery, Fort Johnson and other localities on James island. The iron-clads, anchoring
abreast of Wagner, poured into that devoted but
heroic fort a perfect torrent of the heaviest projectiles.

This bombardment lasted in all its fury without
intermission until the 24th of August, when the practical demolition of Fort Sumter for offensive purposes
was regarded as accomplished. The barbette fire of
that work was wholly silenced and almost entirely
destroyed. From that period Fort Sumter, which
had hitherto rendered essential service in retarding
the operations of the enemy against Battery Wagner,
ceased to be available for that purpose.

The approaches against Battery Wagner — regularly
begun on the 18th of August — were vigorously
pressed by the Federals in the face of every opposition. By the 27th their sappers had advanced to
within nearly an hundred yards of that fort. At this
stage, the fire of Wagner — assisted by the concentric
fire of the James island batteries — despite the regular bombardment from the Federal land and naval
batteries, brought the enterprise of the enemy to a
serious pause. In the language of the officer in command, matters indeed seemed at a stand still, and a
feeling of despondency began to pervade the rank
and file of the army.

In this emergency, as appears by the report of Gen.
Gillmore, two things were resolved, first, to keep
Fort Wagner silent with an overpowering curved
fire from siege and Coehorn mortars, so that the Federal engineers would have only the annoyance of the
more distant Confederate batteries, and secondly, to
breach the bomb-proof shelter with rifle guns, and
thus, depriving the Confederates of their only secure

cover in the work, eventually force them to retire from it.

All the light mortars of the enemy were accordingly moved to the front and placed in position. The heavy rifle guns in the breaching batteries were trained upon the fort, and amply supplied with ordnance stores for prolonged action. The cooperation of the powerful battery of the New Ironsides was secured during the day.

These final preparations for the reduction of Wagner having been fully accomplished, the most terrible bombardment of this unusual siege fairly commenced on the morning of the 5th of September. The artillery practice of the enemy was wonderfully accurate. Such an exhibition of skill in the use of heavy ordnance was probably never before witnessed. "For forty-two consecutive hours the spectacle was one of surpassing sublimity and grandeur. Seventeen siege and Coehorn mortars unceasingly dropped their shells into the work over the heads of the Federal sappers and the guards of the advanced trenches. Thirteen of their heavy Parrott rifles — one hundred, two hundred and three hundred-pounders — pounded away at short though regular intervals at the southwest angle of the bomb-proof; while, during the day time, the New Ironsides with remarkable regularity and precision kept up an incessant stream of eleven-inch shells from her eight gun broadside, ricochetting over the water against the sloping parapet of Wagner, whence, deflected upward with a low remaining velocity, they dropped nearly vertically, exploding within or over the work and rigorously searching every part of it except the subterranean shelters. The calcium lights turned night into day, and while throwing around the Federals an impenetrable obscurity, brilliantly illuminated every object in front, and brought the minutest details of the fort into sharp relief."

Under this tremendous fire of artillery — increased as it was by the concentrated fire of sharp-shooters at every available point — it was impossible for the garrison to man the guns of the fort, or to quit the shelter of the bomb-proof. Wagner therefore became practically silent, only an occasional shot being fired from its heavy guns, and the Confederate sharp-shooters replying as the opportunity offered. Under the favoring influences of this fearful bombardment the Federal sappers prosecuted their labors in comparative security, and with such success, that soon after dark on the night of the 6th of September, they reached and crowned the counterscarp of Wagner near the flank of the sea front. The sufferings of the garrison during this dreadful ordeal can be better imagined than described. Such was the damage caused to the bomb-proof — so completely had the gun chambers been filled with sand — and so seriously had the parapets of the work been affected, with no opportunity afforded for repairs under this ceaseless rain of mortar shells and rifle projectiles, that further efforts to hold the position must certainly eventuate in the capture or destruction of the garrison.

Gallant in the extreme had been its defense, and costly the expenditures and the sacrifices of the enemy. Confederate valor, and the limited means at command could do no more. Environed with severest perils, almost entirely isolated, and apparently in the very jaws of destruction, this brave garrison was yet to be saved. Wagner, in obedience to the orders of Gen. Beauregard was to be evacuated this very night.

Being at the time in command of the light artillery

on James island, and to a certain extent at least an eye witness of the events of that memorable occasion, I trust I will be pardoned for inserting here the following account of the last moments of Wagner, as I penned them in my journal on the morning after its evacuation :

HEAD QUARTERS, LIGHT ARTILLERY,
James Island, September 7th, 1863.

Last night was an historic night in the record of the siege of Charleston. In the afternoon of yesterday it was definitely ascertained that Batteries Wagner and Gregg on Morris island were being rapidly rendered untenable — that the continued damages sustained could not be longer repaired — and that our garrisons were suffering considerably under the heavy and prolonged bombardment. During the preceding forty-eight hours we had lost perhaps one hundred and fifty men in killed and wounded, and the bomb-proofs had suffered most material injury. It was impossible for our troops to live outside of them. The enemy had advanced their works so near, that the Federal flag, as I viewed it from James island, appeared to be planted upon the very edge of the ditch of Wagner. So close were these works, that the guns of the fort could not be sufficiently depressed to bear upon them. In consequence of the ceaseless hurricane of bursting shells, and the proximity of large numbers of Federal sharp-shooters, our men could not show their heads above the parapets to fire upon the working parties who could be distinctly seen, busy as bees, in full view, and just in front of the fort, toiling away with a steadiness and a rapidity truly remarkable. It had become almost, if not quite impossible to provision, reenforce, or relieve the garrison, as the land batteries of the enemy, and the Ironsides and monitors, selecting their positions, kept up an incessant fire not only upon the fort, but also upon the sand hills in its rear, along which any relieving parties would be obliged to advance. Of all these facts the military authorities were fully cognizant, and the evacuation of Morris island became a matter of immediate necessity, not to be accomplished, however, except in the face of dangers many and decided.

Yesterday afternoon we were officially apprised of the fact that the island would be evacuated during the night, and that so soon as the garrisons of Wagner and Gregg had been successfully retired in small boats to be provided for that purpose, and those forts blown up, three rockets would be fired from Fort Johnson, which would be the signal for all our batteries on James island to open upon the enemy on Morris island. If only two rockets should be sent up, it would indicate that our wounded had not been brought away, and in that event our batteries would not open fire.

In order that we might have a full view of everything, about ten o'clock last night, Gen. Taliaferro and myself—with his staff—rode down to Battery Haskell, which commands perhaps the finest prospect of Morris island and the forts. Generals Colquitt and Hagood went to Fort Johnson. When we arrived at Battery Haskell we found all the enemy's batteries, both land and naval, engaged in a very heavy and concentrated fire upon Wagner, and the sand hills lying between Wagner and Gregg. Some attention was occasionally bestowed upon the latter fort. A perfect storm of Parrott, mortar, and nine, and eleven-inch shells was poured upon the devoted head of Wagner. At short ranges Coehorn mortar shells were projected upon the parapets and along the parade of the fort, which, in bursting, set fire to the sand bags, and disseminated a bright light which apparently did not expire with the explosions, but continued burning for several minutes. Calcium lights brought the entire outline of the fort into bold relief—illuminating everything connected with it—while the operations of the enemy were vailed in the thick darkness of the night, relieved only by the lurid flashes of their own artillery. Under such circumstances, and in view of the further fact that the working parties and advanced guards of the enemy were just outside of the fort, its evacuation appeared almost a matter of impossibility. It seemed impracticable to conceal the movement.

That night's bombardment was grand in the extreme. I have

seen nothing of this character more magnificent except the
sublimities of Heaven's own artillery. The earth trembled
with the shock, and the air was filled for hours with the screams
of heavy Parrott projectiles, and the explosions of shells, and
the discharges of ordnance of unusual size and power. The
flight of the mortar shells, like so many shooting stars often
crossing each other's pathway in mid-air, could be distinctly
traced, while the gloom of the night was alternately dissipated
and deepened by the fitful flashes of the guns and the explosions
of countless shells. The silence of the hour was constantly
disturbed by the hoarse thunders and the deep-toned reverbera-
tions of the artillery. Occasionally, discharges of musketry
from the fort could be perceived, and once Wagner fired a
heavy gun. With these exceptions both that battery and Gregg
maintained an absolute silence, enduring without reply this
tremendous bombardment.

For more than fifty days had this earth-work borne the brunt
of unheard of battle, and successfully resisted all the efforts of the
enemy for its reduction — efforts, too, the most extraordinary
in their character, for never before in the annals of sieges had
guns of like calibre, power, and range been employed.

The bombardment continued hour after hour with undimin-
ished fury, our Shell Point batteries, and Batteries Cheves,
Johnson, and Haskell responding slowly, and sometimes with
apparent effect.

Between one and two o'clock on the morning of the 7th, the
moon rose calmly and beautifully from out the sea, bathing the
broad expanse of waters, the adjacent marshes, and the low-
lying islands in a flood of subdued, tranquil light strangely at
variance with the lurid, vengeful glare of the flaming batteries.
For a moment everything would be as noiseless as the grave, and
the heart, lifting itself in sympathy with the peace of nature,
the eye, resting upon the pale moonlight and the softer beams
of the Pleiades, of Jupiter, and of the stars, as unconscious of
human strife they looked down from their homes of tranquil
light, and the ear catching no sound save the voices of the waves
as they chafed with the far off shore, could scarcely realize the

22

fact that while nature slept, man woke to deeds of rude death and direful vengeance. The next moment the air would be filled with the discordant sounds and the wild lights of war; and thus, time and again was presented this antithesis most striking.

Past three o'clock, no signal yet! Four o'clock is almost come, and no announcement that our garrisons have been successfully retired! Nor have the forts been blown up. Everything now is as quiet as death. Firing has entirely ceased on both sides. Just then up goes a rocket from Fort Johnson, and then another, and now a pause! We await the ascent of a third in breathless anxiety. Can it be that in the haste of the evacuation we have been compelled to leave our wounded in the forts to the mercy of the enemy? No, there goes the third rocket announcing the welcome intelligence that our troops are safe, our wounded brought off, and that the evacuation of Morris island has been successfully accomplished. Happy relief, for although we have been compelled to abandon our forts which we have held so long and so manfully, we have saved our garrisons; and what at this juncture is so valuable to the Confederacy as the life of a brave soldier?

And now from Batteries Haskell, Johnson, Cheves and Shell Point our guns open with deafening roar, hurling their projectiles upon Morris island in various directions, and particularly against Forts Wagner and Gregg which we had lately been defending with such heroic determination.

The forts were not blown up as was expected and ordered. The slow matches failed, and the rapid advance of the enemy seriously interfered with the labors of the detachment of twenty men left behind to spike the guns and blow up the magazines. With this exception the evacuation of Morris island was successfully consummated. While it is a source of sincere regret that we have thus been compelled to yield a portion of our soil to the enemy; a locality too, whose possession insures the permanent blockade of Charleston harbor, it is a matter of sincere congratulation that we have been able to retire our troops, under such trying circumstances, from a position so isolated in its character and so thoroughly commanded by the enemy's guns.

The garrisons of Wagner and Gregg were retired by the way of Fort Johnson and Fort Sumter in small boats, which, with one or two exceptions, escaped the vigilance of the enemy.

It does not properly come within the limits of this sketch to pursue further the narrative of the interesting incidents connected with the subsequent operations of the enemy on Morris island and in Charleston harbor, with the gallant repulse by the garrison of Sumter of the assault of the Federal barges on the night of the 9th of September, with the continued bombardments of Sumter, the Sullivan island batteries and the shore batteries on James island, and with the repeated shelling of the city of Charleston. Nor can we pause to dwell upon the peculiar military lessons taught by this the most memorable of modern sieges. It is earnestly hoped that some able pen will present in worthy and reliable form the Confederate memories of this heroic period. Many of them live only in the recollection of the personal actors in that grand drama, and the sooner they are garnered up the better. With the fall of Charleston, and the capture of Richmond, many most valuable records were lost which can never be reproduced; but there are still some floating planks of the shipwrecked vessel which may be recovered from the deluge of time.

During the term of service of the Chatham Artillery upon James island prior to the Florida campaign, the company occupied principally two permanent camps; the first, Camp Simonton not far from Secessionville, and the second, Camp Wheaton, near Royall's place. The *aggregate present for duty*, despite the constant fatigues, exposures and trying climate of this locality, was about one hundred and eleven, and the aggregate present and absent one hundred and forty-nine. One section or the other of the Battery was constantly on picket duty, now at Fort Johnson, now at Freer's cross roads, now at Artillery cross roads, and again in the vicinity of Dill's bluff. The threatening attitude assumed by the enemy kept the Confederate forces on James island in a state of constant anxiety and vigilance. The labors were arduous, and the duties ceaseless, but the Battery responded promptly and cheerfully to every obligation devolved upon it. During this year the Chatham Artillery, in obedience to a general order, was reduced from a six to a four gun battery. This change in the constitution of Confederate batteries, it is believed, was chiefly induced by the deterioration of the rail road transportation of the country. Unable to procure from abroad new and powerful engines, and without the ability to manufacture suitable locomotives at home, and those in general use having lost much of their original power from long wear and tear, it often occurred that with a single locomotive the rail road companies found themselves incapable of transporting in one train with sufficient facility, a six gun battery, with its men, animals, limbers and caissons, forge and ammunition, battery and forage wagons. It was further suggested that a four gun battery was a more convenient organization, and that it constituted a sufficient command for a captain. Whatever may have been the real reasons for this reduction, they were never announced; and the philosophy of the order remains to this day — to many at least — unascertained.

From the 17th of October, 1863, when the Chatham Artillery exchanged its twelve-pounder howitzer section for a section of twelve-pounder Napoleon guns, it remained a four gun twelve-pounder Napoleon battery to the end of the war.

On the fourth of November President Davis visited and inspected the defenses, and reviewed the Confederate forces on James island. On that occasion to the Chatham Artillery was assigned the honor of firing the salute of thirteen guns.

CHAPTER VII.

Services rendered by the Battery in the Florida Campaign.   The Battle
of Ocean Pond, or Olustee Station.

On the night of the 8th of February, 1864, the
Battery was ordered to march from its camp on James
island to the depot of the Charleston and Savannah
rail road, and there take the cars for Savannah.   The
depot was reached at daylight on the morning of the
9th, and the Battery left for Savannah at ten o'clock,
A. M., reaching that city by twelve o'clock, P. M.   The
next day the company marched to its old encampment
at White bluff, where it remained until the morning
of the 12th, when it moved to the depot of the Atlantic
and Gulf rail road and took the cars the same day for
Valdosta, *en route* for Florida.   Arriving at Valdosta
at four o'clock, A. M., on the 13th, the Battery proceeded immediately to Madison, Florida, which point
was reached on the morning of the 14th.   The same
evening it was transported by rail to Lake City, where
it arrived at three o'clock, A. M., on the morning of
the 15th.

At this time the Federal cavalry were advancing
towards Gainesville, and it was feared that they would
continue northward and destroy the Columbia bridge
across the Suwannee river, and perhaps burn Lake
City.   The Chatham Artillery, with the 6th Georgia
Regiment, was ordered to a point some twelve miles
south of Lake City where a strong line of pickets had
been established, and preparations made to resist the
anticipated advance of the Federal cavalry.   There

the Battery remained until the 17th, when it was ordered back to Lake City, and directed to proceed at once to Olustee station, where it arrived at daylight on Thursday morning the 18th of February. Upon reporting for orders to Brig. Gen. Finegan commanding, the Battery was directed to report to Brig. Gen. Colquitt, by whom it was assigned to duty with his brigade. The company bivouacked about half a mile east of the station, immediately in rear of a temporary line of fortifications, all of the pieces being placed in position along the line.

It will be remembered that the Federal expedition under the command of Brig. Gen. Seymour, consisting of twenty steamers of various classes, and eight schooners, left Hilton Head on the morning of the 6th of February, 1864, and arrived without accident at the bar off the mouth of the St. John's river between eight and ten o'clock, A. M., on the 7th. During the afternoon of the same day a landing was effected, and the village of Jacksonville occupied by the United States forces without opposition.

The avowed objects of this expedition were fourfold.

1. To procure an outlet for cotton, lumber, etc., etc.

2. To cut off one of the principal sources of supplies of the commissary department of the Confederacy.

3. To obtain recruits for colored regiments; and,

4. To inaugurate measures for the speedy restoration of the state of Florida to her allegiance to the United States.

To oppose this formidable demonstration there was, at the time, within the limits of the state of Florida but a handful of Confederate troops, consisting chiefly of a few poorly equipped light batteries, a regiment and a battalion of cavalry, and a battalion or two of infantry, and these posted at various detached points.

Rapid concentration was absolutely necessary. Brig. Gen. Colquitt's brigade and the Chatham Artillery from James island, and such troops as could be spared from the military district of Georgia, were ordered by Gen. Beauregard commanding the department, to repair with all possible dispatch to Lake City. By the 18th there was a concentration at Olustee of perhaps forty-six hundred Confederate troops of all arms of the service. The position selected to resist the advance of the enemy was the most judicious afforded for miles along the route chosen by the Federals for the invasion of Florida. Looking in the direction of Jacksonville, on the left was Ocean pond, five miles wide, stretching away for several miles through the low-lying pine-barren, and affording a protection on the left flank of the Confederate position which could only be turned by a detour of perhaps seven or eight miles. On the right lay a swamp which, if not impracticable, would have offered many difficulties in its passage. The only direct approach was by means of the rail road and the wagon road, crossing very near and parallel with each other, along causeways between Ocean pond on the one hand and the swamp on the other. Between the rail road depot and this crossing, and so near as thoroughly to command the latter, field works had been hastily constructed by the Confederates, behind which it was resolved vigorously to dispute the advance of the enemy. Such, in short, was the position selected for the anticipated battle. Both beyond and in rear of this locality, an extended, monotonous, dreary pine-barren stretched in every direction, interrupted here and there by occasional ponds and small water courses, but in no place affording marked physical advantages for impeding the progress of the Federals.

The engagement of the 20th was not fought behind the breast works near Olustee station, or upon the ground originally chosen by the Confederates, but in the open level pine-barren, three miles in advance of that position, and without the slightest premeditation or physical preparation of any kind. In fact, both armies came into collision with each other in mutual surprise, in ignorance of the true status of affairs, upon open ground alike favorable to each, and with no plans or combinations other than such as were born of the moment, and developed by the necessities of the occasion. The battle of Ocean pond, or Olustee station may therefore be regarded as an unusually fair fight, with the preponderance of men and metal in favor of the Federals. All statements by Federal writers to the effect that the United States forces were on this occasion drawn into a carefully planned ambuscade, are entirely without foundation.

The Confederate forces engaged consisted of:

Infantry.

The 1st Georgia Regulars; the 6th, 19th, 23d, 27th, 28th, 32d, and 64th Georgia Regiments; Bonaud's Battalion; and the 2d and 6th Florida Battalions.

Cavalry.

Clinch's Regiment, Georgia Cavalry, and Smith's Regiment Florida Cavalry.

Artillery.

Wheaton's Battery (the Chatham Artillery), four guns; one section of Gamble's Battery, two guns, and one section of Guerard's Battery, two guns ; total, eight guns.

Numbering in the aggregate not more than 4,600 men.[1]

---

[1] This is a most liberal estimate, exceeding the numbers actually engaged.

The Federal forces consisted of:

Infantry.

The 47th, 48th, and 115th New York Regiments; the 7th Connecticut Regiment; the 7th New Hampshire Regiment; the 54th Massachusetts Regiment; the 1st North Carolina Regiment, and the 8th U. S. Volunteer Regiment.

Cavalry, etc.

The 40th Massachusetts Mounted Infantry, and Stevens Battalion of Cavalry.

Artillery.

Elder's Battery, Horse Artillery, four guns; Hamilton's Battery, six guns; Langdon's Battery, four guns, and a section of the 3d Rhode Island Battery, two guns; total, sixteen guns.

Numbering in the aggregate not less than five thousand five hundred men.

On the morning of the 20th the enemy moved from Sanderson in the direction of Olustee in three columns, following the line of the rail road, and the parallel dirt roads.

For the accompanying graphic and accurate account of the battle of Ocean pond, I am indebted to Major George G. Grattan, the accomplished and gallant adjutant general of Colquitt's Brigade, who, during the progress of that memorable engagement, was in all parts of the field, accurately noting the occurrences of the day, and by his personal experience and accustomed bravery contributing most materially to the achievement of that noted victory:

Upon the morning of the 16th of February, 1864, General Colquitt left Savannah with four regiments of his brigade, viz: the 19th, 23d, 27th and 28th Georgia Regiments — the 6th Georgia having already moved forward. We were transported in the cars of the Atlantic and Gulf rail road to Station Number 9, arriving there in the night. The next morning early, we commenced marching across the country to Madison, Florida, taking with us no baggage except our cooking utensils, and such as the men could carry in their knapsacks. We halted in the evening at a river some ten or twelve miles from Madison, and went into camp. About twelve o'clock at night Gen. Colquitt received a dispatch from Gen. Finegan stating that the enemy were advancing, and requesting him to move on as rapidly as possible. Gen. Colquitt immediately ordered his command forward, and we reached Madison the next morning at sunrise, having marched over thirty miles in twenty-four hours without leaving a man by the road side. Trains of cars were in readiness at Madison, and we moved on so soon as the troops could be put aboard. As we passed through Lake City we were joined by the 6th Georgia Regiment. We arrived at Olustee station the same evening, February 18th, and there learned that the reported advance of the enemy consisted of a body of cavalry which had turned towards the south, after destroying some depots, etc. During the entire day after our arrival at Olustee we were quiet, and the troops enjoyed a good opportunity for rest. On the morning of the 20th, Gen. Finegan having received some information from the front, sent forward the cavalry under the command of Col. Smith, with what specific instructions I am unacquainted. Later in the morning the 64th Georgia—Col. Evans commanding—was sent out as a support for the cavalry. Soon after mid-day Gen. Colquitt received a written order from Gen. Finegan to take the 6th and 28th Georgia Regiments, the 6th Florida Battalion and two guns of Gamble's Florida Battery, and proceed to the front, and drive the enemy's *cavalry* from the rail road which they were reported to be tearing up at a point some distance below Olustee. We had not started from the station before Gen. Colquitt received another order directing Col. Harrison to report to him with the 32d Georgia and the 1st Georgia Regulars of his command. Capt. Wheaton's Battery (the Chatham Artillery), and the 23d Georgia Regiment of Colquitt's Brigade were at the same time ordered to the front. Gen. Colquitt moved forward at once with the first detachment which was just ready, and ordered the other commands to follow on rapidly so soon as they could be formed.

After marching about four miles from Olustee we perceived the 64th Georgia Regiment drawn up in a square, just in rear of the point where the wagon road crosses the rail road. Gen. Colquitt galloped ahead, and inquiring the condition of affairs, was informed by Lieut. Col. Barrow that our cavalry were retiring before the enemy. Looking through the trees he could see a column on each side of the road moving in rapid retreat, and could hear the firing of the enemy as they followed on behind. Gen. Colquitt then ordered Col. Evans to form his regiment in line of battle on the left of the road. Ordering up the section of Gamble's Battery he instructed it to take a position at the crossing, and directed Col. Neal commanding the 19th Georgia to form immediately on the right of the guns. The 6th and 28th Georgia Regiments were formed on the left of the 64th, and a staff officer was dispatched to the cavalry directing it to form on the flanks. Accordingly Col. Smith moved to the right flank with his regiment, and Col. Clinch to the left with his.

The front being thus cleared, a regiment of the enemy's cavalry which had been dismounted — and which as skirmishers had been following our cavalry very closely — now pushing forward, saw our troops in the act of forming line of battle, and commenced a very brisk fire upon us. Being armed with long range *Spencer rifles*, their fire was very effective, and threw some of our troops into considerable confusion. Lieut. Col. Barrow of the 64th Georgia was killed, and Col. Evans and Major —— of the same regiment were both wounded. That regiment being thus left without a field officer, and having never before been in action, became somewhat broken, but the coolness of the 28th Georgia restored these men to confidence, and many of them rallied and fought through the action. Captain Gamble's men being raw troops were considerably excited by the suddenness with which they had been thrown into action. Gen. Colquitt finding that the enemy were in strong force — and in fact seeing their dark lines of infantry forming in the distance — sent back a staff officer to hasten forward the rest of his troops, and to request reenforcements from Gen. Finegan. While we had been thus forming our line of battle the enemy had been forming theirs. They soon opened upon us with a battery of six guns. and the musketry fire became very brisk. The 6th Florida Battalion, under the command of Major Byrd, coming up at this juncture, was ordered to take position on the right of the 19th Georgia, and the men moved to their place under a severe fire with perfect steadiness, notwithstanding the fact that it was the first time they had ever been engaged.

Our line now advanced steadily upon the enemy who had been firing at long range. The Chatham Artillery coming up, was ordered to take position in the centre, one gun of Gamble's section having been disabled by a shot from the enemy, and the horses and men of the other not being in a condition to move. Under the direction of Capt. Wheaton, the men of his battery managed their pieces with great coolness and effect. Col. Harrison's detachment arriving on the ground, he was instructed to form on the left of the road, and the 6th Georgia was moved by the flank to the left to give front for the formation of the 32d Georgia, the 23d Georgia, and the 1st Georgia Regulars. While this change was being made, Gen. Colquitt sent orders to the officers commanding the cavalry to press upon the enemy's flanks, while he charged them in front. Col. Smith dismounted his men and moved them out as skirmishers, but being badly armed and poorly drilled, they failed to attack with effect. Col. Clinch attempted a movement on horse, but becoming involved in a marsh was prevented from accomplishing anything of moment.

About this time Gen. Colquitt received another written order from Gen. Finegan sending forward all the troops at Olustee except two guns of Gamble's Battery, and a small battalion, and assigning Gen. Colquitt to the command of the *whole*. A member of Gen. Finegan's staff, Capt. Tucker, also rode up and stated that Gen. Finegan desired Gen. Colquitt, if hard pressed, to fall back to the works at Olustee station. Gen. Colquitt —

aware of the great danger which would be incurred in attempting such a movement under existing circumstances, and reposing every confidence in his troops, who were fighting with a steadiness never excelled — ordered a general charge. With a shout which rose far above the roll of the musketry and the thunders of the artillery, our men dashed upon the enemy. Their line was soon broken, and five of their six guns in position immediately in our front were captured. The enemy were now virtually routed. Our line, which had been somewhat broken in the charge, was reformed to press on, when it was ascertained that our ammunition was almost exhausted. We had been unable to take our ammunition wagons to Florida, and the ordnance officer at Olustee had been instructed to send ammunition down by the rail road in the event of any action, which we hardly anticipated when leaving the station. Soon after the commencement of the engagement, however, Gen. Colquitt had dispatched his ordnance officer to hasten up the supply; but owing to the disordered condition of things there, the cars were delayed for some time, and we were compelled to remain for half an hour in front of an enemy three times our numerical strength, without a supply of ammunition. The situation was indeed a very critical one, and nothing but the calm courage of our men enabled us to hold our ground. A line of skirmishers was sent forward, supplied with what cartridges were left, and with such as could be found in the boxes of the dead Federals, of whom — happily for us — there was quite a number lying upon the portion of the field now occupied by us. The artillery, reenforced by a section of Capt. Guerard's Battery under Lieut. Gignilliat, kept up a very steady and effective fire, and in a great measure assisted in holding the enemy in check.

At length, after a period of intense suspense, the expected car arrived, and never was bread more eagerly snatched by starving wretches than were the cartridges seized by the men as the boxes were broken open along the line.

Just as the ammunition-car arrived, Bonaud's Battalion reached the scene of action, and was moved at once to the skirmish line directly in front of our centre, where it sustained

a very heavy fire while our men were being supplied with
ammunition. Col. Zachry now arrived on the field with the
27th Georgia and the 2d Florida Battalion, and took the position in line vacated by the 6th and 32d Georgia Regiments,
which were moved to the left by a circuit to come in upon the
enemy's right flank which rested behind a fence in rear of a
small cabin in the woods.

The Federals, encouraged by our inaction, had formed a
double line of battle, with a strong force of negro troops upon
their left front. They had also put in motion a body of reenforcements, which had just arrived on the ground, to make an
attack upon our left flank. By this time our troops were again
prepared for action, and Gen. Colquitt ordered the whole line
to press forward in front, while the 6th and 32d Georgia Regiments came in upon the right flank of the enemy. For a while
the firing was very rapid, and the position then occupied by
the enemy could, after the engagement was over, be distinctly
traced by the dead left upon the field. Col. Zachry with his
fresh troops was moving on with great determination just as
the 6th and 32d Georgia closed in upon the enemy's flank,
which soon began to waver, and gradually giving back, the
whole line was broken, and our men rushed forward to follow
up the rout which now became complete. After following on
for several miles, darkness overtook us, and we were ordered to
halt. Immediately upon the commencement of the rout Gen.
Colquitt had ordered the cavalry to the front in pursuit, but
they did not proceed far beyond the point where the infantry
halted, when the officer in command returned and reported that
the enemy had gone into camp and appeared to be in good
order. The officer stated that he had himself gone near enough
to see the troops, and to hear the commands as they were halted
and ordered to stack arms. By this time Gen. Finegan had
arrived in front, and assumed command. He now directed
Gen. Colquitt to leave one regiment in front as an advanced
guard, and to march the rest of his troops back to camp at
Olustee station. We did not commence the pursuit of the
enemy until late the next day, or the morning of the day sub-

sequent. The Federals had been completely routed, and did not pause in their precipitate retreat until safe under the shelter of their gun-boats at Jacksonville. Nothing but our inaction and the inefficiency of our cavalry saved the entire Federal army from capture. At Baldwin they destroyed a large amount of ordnance and other stores, because, in their haste, they were unable to carry them off.

*   *   *   *   *   *   *   *

I am well assured that Gen. Colquitt had no anticipation of a serious engagement until after the commencement of the fight, and I believe that Gen. Finegan had no information of the advance of any infantry force. All the movements upon the field were directed by Gen. Colquitt.

*   *   *   *   *   *   *   *

The enemy seemed as much surprised as we were at the precipitation of the engagement. They were on the march to Tallahassee, and did not expect to meet any infantry force before reaching Lake City — at least so the prisoners reported. I take it that the engagement was a mutual surprise, upon perfectly fair and open ground. Except in numbers it was the fairest battle I saw or heard of during the whole war. Col. Harrison, after arriving upon the field, was instructed to take charge of the left wing of our forces, which he did; and, in the discharge of the duties devolved upon him, gained the confidence and respect of the troops under his command by his bearing in the fight. It does not become me to particularize officers, but I cannot forbear expressing my admiration of the conduct of Col. Zachry of the 27th Georgia, Col. Neal of the 19th Georgia, Major Banning of the 28th Georgia, and Capt. Wheaton of the Chatham Artillery.

Capt. Wheaton has kindly furnished the following account of the part borne by his Battery during this important engagement:

At twelve o'clock M. on the 20th of February, 1864, one section of our Battery was ordered to the front in company

with the 6th Georgia Regiment. As we proceeded, we were
joined by the 32d Georgia and the 1st Georgia Regulars. After
we had advanced about two miles, we were greeted by a shot from
one of the enemy's rifle field pieces, which, passing over our heads,
killed a private of the 32d Georgia directly in our rear. This
was the first shot fired from the Federal artillery. At this
moment a courier from Gen. Colquitt arrived with orders for
me to move my Battery out of the road, and to report in person
to him. This I did, and received instructions from the general
to post my guns one hundred yards to the right of Gamble's
Battery. At this time there was some artillery and musketry
firing from the enemy, but it had not become general. Our
troops were resting upon the ground, the left of the line terminating near the rail road track. Gamble's Battery was in the
rear of the infantry, its left about thirty feet from the dirt road
which crossed the rail road diagonally some fifty yards in front.
My orders were to occupy the position designated, and to open
fire so soon as we came into battery (the enemy could then be
seen about a thousand yards distant), and to advance or retire with
the infantry, keeping my Battery dressed on Gamble's Battery.

Gen. Colquitt said to me, " Captain, use your own judgment
in directing your fire, unless otherwise ordered. I expect a good
report from your Battery. Be sure and keep your men well in
hand." My reply was, " General, I will do my best." I then
galloped to my command and we moved immediately to the
point specified. As we were coming into battery, the infantry
were forming line of battle. Gamble's Battery fired the first
shot. We opened at once, directing our fire at the enemy's
infantry. The firing on both sides had now become general.
After firing some five or six rounds from each piece, finding
that the infantry had advanced and was still advancing, I
thought it time to move my section further to the front. Looking to the left to see where Gamble's Battery was, I discovered
that it was in great confusion. The horses had become unman-
ageable, and some of them were running down the road to the
rear at the top of their speed, with the limbers and without
drivers. That battery had ceased firing. At that moment

24

I was ordered to occupy a position directly in front of where
Gamble's Battery had been posted, and to keep my Battery
as near the centre of the infantry line as practicable, moving
to the front as the infantry advanced.   Limbering up we
moved at a brisk trot to the point designated, and opened
fire rapidly.   Here there was hard fighting, and for some time
it was difficult to say which side had the advantage.   The
enemy had sixteen pieces of artillery engaged.   On our side,
our section was the only artillery then in action.   Thinking it
time to have our other section ordered up, as Gen. Colquitt
was near by, I sent a courier to him and requested permission
to send for it.   The request was granted.   The infantry fighting here was magnificent.   Nothing could withstand it.   The
enemy held on for a time, but finally gave way, and we advanced
some two hundred yards.   Here the enemy again resisted stub-
bornly.   Their batteries were only about five hundred yards
distant.   Gen. Colquitt came in person to our section and
ordered me to concentrate its fire upon one of the Federal
batteries on our right, and to keep it on that battery as long as
I could do so with safety to our infantry who had been directed
to advance and take the battery.   I directed First Sergeant Miller
(I had no commissioned officer with me, Lieut. Palmer being
with the other section at Olustee station, and Lieutenants
Askew and Hendry being absent on leave), to superintend
personally the fuzing of the shells.   We soon got the range,
and did good execution.   The infantry advanced, and in a short
time captured two of the Federal guns.   On this part of the line
the enemy gave way badly, but in the centre and on our left
they were still offering a vigorous resistance.   Similar attention
was paid to their artillery on another portion of the line.   The
infantry charged, and the enemy retreated at all points, leaving
three more of their pieces in our possession.   We advanced
rapidly, unlimbered and fired a few shots, and then advancing
again went into battery at the last position which we occupied
until the close of the engagement.   Here reenforcements reached
the enemy, and it was all that we could do to hold our own.   Just
then our left section arrived on the field.   It did not come a

minute too soon. The right section had expended nearly all
its ammunition except canister, which we had not used because
the ground was so thickly wooded. We could discover no
favorable results from the few rounds which had been fired,
while the effect of solid shot and shells was very apparent. The
infantry had also expended the ammunition from their cartridge
boxes, and from some unexplained cause the ordnance wagons
were not at hand. This was a trying season. The infantry
acted nobly, but on the right was forced to give back a little.
At this time our Battery was as far in advance as any part of
the line, and rendered efficient service. Our fire was directed
against such portions of the enemy's line as appeared to be causing most damage. Sometimes it was concentrated on one given
point, and again it was distributed as circumstances seemed to
render it advisable.

Here Gen. Colquitt rode up to the Battery and ordered me to
retire my guns a little. I replied, " General, I think we can
hold on five minutes. By that time the ordnance wagons may
be up, which will change the aspect of affairs." He replied,
that he was afraid we would lose our pieces. I answered that
if he would allow me, I would take the risk ; that I could rely
upon my men. The general responded, " Very well, but be
sure and save your guns." Soon after, the 27th Georgia and
Bonaud's Battalion were announced as coming up. The ammunition arrived at nearly the same time. This encouraged us all,
and the fighting on our part was renewed with vigor. I shall
never forget this moment. The annals of the war do not record
any more heroic fighting than was done by the 27th Georgia.
That regiment moved like a wall of fire, and every inch it
gained, it held. Bonaud's Battalion also acted nobly. In fact,
all the troops showed the right metal. The contest was desperate, and for some time the result was doubtful. At length the
enemy's left began to waver. As they were making a strenuous effort to keep their left centre up to the mark, a solid
shot from one of our pieces cut down a large tree which fell
directly in their midst. From the confusion thus caused, that
portion of the line — severely pressed as it was by our advanc-

ing infantry — never recovered. In a conversation which I had with a Federal officer, since the termination of the war, who was present on this occasion, he remarked that in his judgment the falling of that tree just at that particular juncture decided the fate of the day on the left of their line. On the enemy's right, a regiment of mounted infantry and a battery of horse artillery united with the infantry in the effort to retrieve what had been lost on the left, and there were some instances of gallantry on the part of Federal officers which could scarcely be excelled.

A section of Capt. Guerard's Battery, under the command of Lieut. Gignilliat, arrived upon the field, and by direction of Gen. Colquitt was posted immediately upon our left. It came most opportunely, as we had expended all of our solid shot and shells. We fired seventy rounds from Lieut. Gignilliat's chests. By this time the enemy had given way at all points, and the field was won. We limbered up and went in pursuit, but did not get another shot. The command was halted about twilight, and we were ordered to collect such of the enemy's artillery as was left on the field, and to return with it to our bivouac at Olustee station. We took back three of the five captured pieces. A large number of our men were engaged all night and the day following in gathering ammunition and artillery stores from the field, and in taking care of the wounded.

The Battery lost not a single man, killed, and those who were wounded, were not seriously wounded. The pieces and gun carriages, limbers and caissons were frequently struck. There were many narrow escapes, and that no member of the company was killed appears an absolute miracle.

In the absence of specific returns, it is difficult to present an entirely reliable statement of the aggregate losses sustained in this action. The Confederate forces engaged did not number more than forty-six hundred men of all arms. This is not only a liberal but an outside estimate. Federal correspondents admit that five thousand men were brought into

action on their side. It is believed from the indications of the field, the report of prisoners, and other
facts connected with the history of the invasion, that
this estimate is too small by perhaps fifteen hundred
men.   In the matter of field artillery the enemy held
vastly the preponderance, both as to the number and
calibre of the pieces engaged.   Early in the action
Gamble's section became disabled and withdrew.
Wheaton's right section was the only artillery then on
the field on the Confederate side.   It was subsequently
reenforced by the left section, and toward the heel of
the engagement, one section of Guerard's Battery
came into action.   While, therefore, the Confederates
had nominally eight guns in action, in reality Wheaton's right section was the only artillery actively
engaged during the entire battle, and for some time
was the only Confederate artillery on the field.   Sixteen pieces of Federal artillery were in battery during
the continuance of the combat.

From the most authentic sources of information,
the Confederate losses may be stated at ninety-five
killed, and eight hundred and thirty wounded.   Large
numbers of the latter were so slightly wounded that
they returned to duty in a very short time, and others
did not leave their commands at all.   Nearly four
hundred Federals were left dead upon the field, and
we captured about an equal number, most of whom
were severely wounded.   It is admitted by the enemy
that over five hundred of their wounded were sent off
by transports from Jacksonville, and the aggregate
loss sustained in the battle of Olustee has been stated,
by at least one of the Federal letter writers, to have
been not less than nineteen hundred.   It would probably be not an over estimate to record it at two
thousand.   Certain it is, that the effect of this disas-

trous defeat was emphatically to put an end to all
Federal operations in Florida, and to hurl back in fear
and rapid retreat the remnant of a proud invading
army, confident of success, within the range of the
gun-boats whose batteries had so recently protected
its landing.

As material trophies of the conflict, the Confederates captured three twelve-pounder Napoleon guns
of Langdon's Battery, 1st U. S. Artillery, two ten-
pounder Parrott rifles of Hamilton's Battery, 3d
U. S. Artillery, more than three thousand stand of
small arms — among them, nearly two hundred Spencer rifles — a large amount of ammunition, and some
quarter master's stores.

To the Chatham Artillery — as a mark of the commanding general's appreciation of their gallant and
efficient conduct during the engagement — was assigned
a section of the captured twelve-pounder Napoleon
guns. These guns with their battle-scarred carriages
the company retained with feelings of special pride,
as a component part of their battery during the
remainder of the war. They were finally surrendered
at Greensboro, North Carolina, in April, 1865, upon
the occasion of the surrender of the army of Gen.
Joseph E. Johnston.

The Chatham Artillery went into the engagement
with an aggregate present of one hundred and eleven
men, as appears by the morning report, and the
conduct of officers and men during the entire action
was such as to elicit the universal commendation of
their copatriots in arms.[1] In the history of this time

---

[1] After the engagement, as the Battery was returning from the vic-
torious field, it was lustily cheered again and again by the men of
Colquitt's Brigade, than whom Georgia never sent braver or truer sons
to battle.

honored organization the memories of this illustrious
day will be cherished with emotions of peculiar pride;
and as often as its heroic incidents are recounted, so
often will the heart be lifted up in gratitude to the
God of battles, for the broad mantle of His protection
with which on that day He covered the heads of the
brave men of this Battery.

The legitimate fruits of this victory—which should
have been nothing less than the capture of the entire
Federal force—were not reaped on account of the
inefficiency of the cavalry. Had the enemy been at
all pressed during their precipitate retreat upon Jacksonville, immediate and unconditional surrender would
have been yielded. Their own accounts prove this,
and their surprise was that they were permitted to
escape. The entire line of march from Olustee battle-
field to Jacksonville was filled with the evidences of
the most abandoned flight.

The true hero of the battle of Ocean pond, or
Olustee station, was Brig. Gen. Colquitt.[1]

The second day after the engagement, the following
congratulatory orders were issued:

HEAD QUARTERS, DISTRICT E, FLORIDA,
February 22, 1864.

GENERAL ORDER No. ..

I. The brigadier general commanding thanks the officers and
men of this command for their bravery and admirable conduct
in the engagement with the enemy at Ocean pond on the 20th
inst. The signal victory which their valor achieved, will be of
great service to their country. To the courage of the men of

---

[1] For the accompanying excellent sketch of the battle field of Ocean
pond, I am indebted to Lieut. Miller B. Grant, of the Confederate States
Engineer Corps, whose name, and skill, and indefatigable labors will
always be honorably associated with the proud memories of the Florida
campaign.

Georgia and Florida is this victory due, and to their states will its results more especially enure.

II. The brigadier general commanding acknowledges the distinguished services of Brig. Gen. A. H. Colquitt commanding in the front, to whom much of the success of the battle is due, and of Col. George P. Harrison, commanding 2d brigade, both of whom conducted themselves with the highest degree of courage and ability.

III. The brigadier general commanding also returns his thanks to Brig. Gen. Gardner, commanding Dist. Mid. Fla. and the officers of his staff, for their presence and assistance during the engagement.

IV. The conduct of both officers and men will be noticed in detail in the report of the brigadier general commanding to department head quarters.

By order of

BRIG. GEN. FINEGAN,

W. Call, A. A. G.

The Chatham Artillery moved on with the army of East Florida in its advance towards Jacksonville, and formed a component part of it until the 19th of April. It having been ascertained that reenforcements were arriving in Jacksonville, and that the approaches to that village were guarded both by Federal gun-boats and land batteries, it was resolved to keep the enemy closely invested and await future developments. Accordingly the general encampment of the Confederate forces was located along the line of McGirts creek, some nine miles below Baldwin in the direction of Jacksonville, and immediately upon the rail road. This encampment was subsequently protected by the construction of substantial defensive works, and received the name of Camp Milton. On the morning of the 1st of March, a detachment from the army — of which the Chatham Artillery formed a component part — under the command of Col. Zachry, was sent

forward to drive in the advanced guards of the enemy
and establish our picket line several miles in advance
of the position then occupied, thus putting a greater
space between the two armies, and materially conduc-
ing to the security of our own. Before this advance
the enemy's pickets and advanced guards retreated.
In this they were very materially influenced by several
well directed shots from Wheaton's Battery. Our
forces pressed on, passing Camp Finegan and encountering no serious opposition until they reached a small
creek beyond. In crossing this, the enemy, considerably reenforced, inflicted a loss upon us of ten killed
and twenty or thirty wounded. Here the Chatham
Artillery shelled the enemy heavily, and the crossing
was effected under the cover of this fire, the enemy
again continuing their retreat. Our lines having been
sufficiently advanced, the detachment returned to
Camp Milton.

With the cavalry well in advance, the army rested
quietly at Camp Milton, and the Federals — confined
within the limits of Jacksonville and its vicinity —
busied themselves rather with matters looking to their
personal safety, than with preparations for a renewal
of their boasted march through Florida. An expedition was sent up the St. John's, but it eventuated only
in an early recall, and the loss of two of the steam
transports engaged, which were blown up by our torpedoes. The Federals lingered about Jacksonville
for some time, but the memories of the bloody defeat
at Ocean Pond were too recent to permit the hazard
of a second engagement, and they eventually entirely
abandoned the hope of rendering Florida loyal, and
returned their forces to the Carolina coast. Without
entering upon a detailed account of the duties performed by the Chatham Artillery while stationed at

Camp Milton, we may state in general terms that the
Battery was parked with the rest of the artillery of
the army — numbering some twenty pieces — under
the command of Lieut. Colonel C. C. Jones, Jr., chief
of artillery, and that it cheerfully and efficiently responded to every obligation devolved upon it, whether
upon picket duty in front with the cavalry, in the construction of temporary fortifications for the protection
of Camp Milton, or in the performance of the general
duties of the camp and the drill.

CHAPTER VIII.

Return to James Island.   Affair of the 2d of July, etc.

On the 19th of April, 1864, the Chatham Artillery left Camp Milton, and marching across the country *via* Trader's hill, took the cars of the Atlantic and Gulf rail road at Station Number 9, and thence proceeding *via* Savannah, reached James island on the 30th. Here the company was associated with Capt. Blake's Battery in a temporary battalion under the command of Capt. Wheaton, the senior officer.

The services performed by the company during the summer were arduous and unceasing. Half the Battery was upon guard or picket duty every night. A great deal of courier duty was demanded of the company on account of the want of cavalry and the paucity of troops generally on the island. Skirmishes with the enemy were not infrequent.

Alluding to the condition and engagements of his Battery, Captain Wheaton writes under date of May 31st, 1864 :

Our duties here are severe. We furnish an average of twenty-four men daily as guards at head quarters, at the signal station, at Dill's bluff bridge, at the ordnance and commissary depots, and as mounted couriers at the different posts on the island. Besides, we send a section to Fort Johnson every night on picket duty. These details, in connection with our camp guard, embrace the whole company. Men who come off guard in the morning, go on picket in the evening ; and with all this I have never known the men more cheerful, or apparently better satisfied. They appreciate the fact that the duty is necessary, and perform it willingly. We are located about one hundred yards below the camp we occupied last season, on the ground immediately south of the road leading from our old camp to Artillery cross roads; and notwithstanding our hard duty, are more comfortable in every particular than at any time since we left White bluff. The men are in snug cabins; we have a good stable for our horses, harness racks, and a guard house and forage house, all complete. We have about one hundred and thirty men in camp. The general health is good. It is unusual to have more than seven on the sick list at one time, and often we do not have more than two or three. In all respects I consider the company in fully as good condition as at any time during the war. Our horses — except the few we use on courier duty — have improved, and are now in fine working order. Capt. Blake's company is camped with us, and we do the duty in common, furnishing thirty-eight men daily for guard duty outside of our camp, and sending a section to Fort Johnson, and another section to a point known as River's causeway on picket every night.

There is not to my knowledge, at present, an infantry soldier on the island. Frederick's Regiment of Heavy Artillery, and Manigault's three siege artillery companies are doing duty as infantry. We have also about three hundred and fifty dismounted cavalry, portions of two regiments recently returned from Virginia to be remounted. A part of the 1st Regiment Regular Artillery is on duty at Fort Johnson, and the Lucas Battalion is stationed on the Stono. You will easily see from your knowledge of our long lines, that we have plenty of employment for every man. The enemy has made two demonstrations on the lower and western part of the island recently, driving in our pickets, but gaining no permanent advantage. They retired as soon as our forces were concentrated. In an emergency we muster quite a respectable little army. We recently had twelve companies of firemen from Charleston, all armed, two companies of cadets from the Citadel academy, and various volunteer organizations. We can make a good fight, with chances

for success in an open field; and with the advantages of our
fortifications I think we can hold at bay any force the enemy
probably can bring against us.   The Federals continue to shell
the city, but cause little damage.   They also shell the works
on this island daily, but without effect.[1]

*   *   *   *   *   *   *   *

Captain Wheaton thus describes the part sustained
by the Chatham Artillery in the early part of July:

On the morning of the 2d of July the enemy rushed on us
in considerable force, driving in our advanced pickets and capturing a section of Capt. Blake's guns on picket at River's
causeway.   Lieut. DeLorme, who was in command of the section,
fought his guns admirably, and would probably have saved
them, but for the desertion of a wheel driver who, at a most
critical moment, sprang from his horse and fled to the enemy.   At
the same time Lieut. DeLorme's horse was shot from under him,
and some confusion was thereby created.   He was obliged to
leave his pieces, but brought off his limbers and horses.   It is
proper to state that the men Lieut. DeLorme had with him as

---

[1] At half-past one o'clock on the morning of the 2d of June, 1864, a
boat expedition under the command of Lieut. Pelot, of the Confederate
states navy, after a desperate hand to hand conflict of some fifteen
minutes, succeeded in boarding and capturing the United States
steamer Water Witch in Ossabaw sound.   This vessel formed one of the
blockading squadron on the coast of Georgia, and at the time of her
capture was armed with a battery of four guns.   Her crew consisted
of eighty-two men.   The attacking party numbered eighty, in seven
barges.   This gallant exploit, which should be specially remembered
among the daring achievements of this heroic period, was accomplished
at the cost of the life blood of the brave young commander, who was
the first to gain the deck of the Water Witch, and there fell, shot
through the heart, while with his own hand contending most valiantly
with the enemy.   In this engagement the Confederates lost six killed
and twelve wounded.   The enemy's loss consisted of two killed and
fifteen wounded, among the latter, Lieut. Pendergrast commanding.
Eighty Federal prisoners were captured with the steamer, her battery,
and entire equipment.

cannoneers on this occasion, were chiefly recruits fresh from the
conscript camp, who had not been with the company long enough
to be thoroughly instructed in their duties. His only mistake —
if he did commit a mistake — was that he did not retire his
section a moment sooner. His only support consisted of fifteen
men from the South Carolina siege train acting as infantry. All
that could be done was done, but it was impossible for this
small force to drive back three full regiments of infantry
advancing in three separate columns. From prisoners, subsequently captured, we learned that between ninety and one
hundred of the enemy were killed and wounded in front of
Lieut. DeLorme's section. Fourteen of their dead were lying
unburied when the enemy retired across this causeway the
Sunday following. At the same time that this attack was
made at River's causeway, the enemy pushed forward a force at
Grimball's causeway and drove our pickets across. While
retaining possession of that causeway, they deployed two other
columns to the right and left of the causeway, crossed the
marsh, and forced back our reserves. At this juncture our
Battery was ordered to the front to support our pickets, and
check the advance of the enemy. We started from Battery
Number 2, near the church, down the Grimball road, and
moving rapidly soon took a position in rear of our skirmish line,
and opening upon the enemy in a short time brought them to a
halt. They had no artillery with them, but several rocket
batteries; which, however, produced no effect other than fright-
ening horses. We held our position here all day, firing as
often as the Federals showed themselves, and shelling their
lines. We soon silenced their rocket batteries and their infantry fire, and were only annoyed by their sharp-shooters.
Thus passed the first day, and I will add the hottest day in
point of temperature I ever experienced. The sun was terrible,
and we had to take its rays in full force. During the day the
enemy had but one gun-boat in the Stono. It kept up a con-
tinual shelling from morning until evening, without, however,
causing any damage. Soon after dark Gen. Taliaferro, fearing
that the enemy might by a sudden dash capture our Battery,

ordered it within the lines. The entire infantry force which could be spared from the guns along the lines, did not on this day exceed three hundred men. Saturday night a portion of the 32d Georgia arrived, and the garrisons at the fixed batteries on the island were literally robbed so that we could muster an available, movable infantry force of some six hundred men. With this force the general decided, if possible, to drive the enemy across the marsh back upon the peninsula which they had been occupying, and from which their recent advance had been made. The column moved before daylight under command of Col. Harrison, with one section of Blake's Battery and one section of our Battery. As the ground between the two causeways was impracticable for the movements of artillery, we selected positions whence we could cover, as far as possible, the field of operations. The infantry deployed and swept in line of battle over the space recently occupied by the enemy; but they had evacuated in the night, and our picket line was reestablished on this side of the marsh. This was also a terribly hot day. A number of men were sun-struck, and others so affected by the heat that they fainted. The enemy had, during the day, two monitors, the Pawnee, and six gun-boats in the Stono, and such a shelling as they gave us it has never been my fortune to undergo. They did not discover us until about nine o'clock in the morning, and then they opened all their broadsides upon us with solid shot, shell and grape; and I can assure you they made it warm for us. My orders were to support Col. Harrison and to fire on the enemy wher-ever seen. We endured this shelling for two hours, when hearing nothing from Col. Harrison, and seeing nothing of the enemy, I decided to send our caissons to the rear. This drew off a portion of the fire of the Federal fleet, but still it was main-tained very heavily. At twelve o'clock we were ordered to retire.

*　　*　　*　　*　　*　　*　　*　　*

From this time until the enemy evacuated the island, we kept a portion of our pieces in position behind the lines, with our horses harnessed. This continued for the space of ten days. We were continuously on duty; now at night on picket duty in front, and now in reserve behind the lines, ready to move at a moment's notice.

On the eleventh day we returned to camp. The exposure, want of sleep, and intense heat caused a great deal of sickness among the men.

*   *   *   *   *   *   *   *

The powerful accumulations of Federal forces in Virginia and in Northern Georgia had necessitated the strongest possible concentration of Confederate troops and materials of war in their respective fronts to oppose their devastating advance. For this purpose every soldier who could possibly be spared from other quarters was ordered to one or the other of these vital points. The consequence was that James island, in common with other localities along the coast, was well nigh stripped of its defenders. Under such circumstances the advantage of the new line on James island — the right of which rested on the Stono river at Battery Pringle, and the left on Battery Lamar near Secessionville, these extremes being connected by intermediate detached field .works of more than usual strength, well armed, mutually supporting each other, and united by curtains affording ample protection for infantry, and with ramps for field artillery at convenient distances — shortening as it did the defensive line, and rejecting that portion of the island most accessible to the approach of the enemy, and consequently demanding a much smaller number of men for its defense than the old lines required, was most apparent. There can be no question of the fact, that the knowledge of the existence and the strength of this new line deterred the enemy from an advance which would otherwise have been fairly provoked by the meagreness of the forces to whom for months was confided the defense of James island.

During this summer, Capt. Wheaton being in command of the battalion formed as before stated, the immediate command of the Battery devolved upon Senior First Lieutenant Thomas A. Askew. About the 1st of September a section of the Chatham Artillery under the command of Lieut. Palmer was ordered to the Race course near the city of Charleston to assist in guarding the Federal prisoners there confined. It remained on this duty until those prisoners were sent to Florence. To add to the disagreeable nature of this duty, the yellow fever made its appearance among the troops and in the city of Charleston; but the same kind Providence which had hitherto watched over, and in a marked manner preserved their lives in seasons of peculiar peril and exposure, on this occasion also mercifully shielded the members of this detachment from the fatal influences of the pestilence. Lieut. Hendry was also on duty with this section while upon this detached service.

On the 5th of December the Battery was relieved from duty on James island, and ordered to occupy the field works at the Combahee river ferry covering the approach to Green Pond station on the Charleston and Savannah rail road. The change was a very pleasant one to the men. The rations issued on James island had of late been so meagre in quantity, and of such an inferior quality, that they were barely sufficient to satisfy the cravings of hunger. There was nothing in them to provoke an appetite. A little sorghum syrup, some musty corn meal, and blue beef once a week, comprised the sum total of the rations issued. Forage for horses also had long since ceased to be adequate. Here, however, we found a region abounding in poultry, pork, beef, rice, and sweet potatoes. Wild ducks congregated in great numbers

26

in the vicinity of the encampment, and were readily killed. Many planters were removing their negroes to safer localities, and their generous stores were, in many instances, freely bestowed upon the members of the Battery. To Mr. Walter Blake, to Mr. Lowndes, and to others, the company was indebted for special favors.

Anticipating the early advent of Gen. Sherman's army on the coast — alive to the importance of opening in advance, if possible, an avenue of facile communication between it and an expectant fleet — and anxious to prevent the rapid concentration, upon an emergency, of the garrisons of Savannah and Charleston, by occupying the Charleston and Savannah rail road — the only direct and rapid means of communication between the two cities — the Federals were assembling their forces at several points in considerable numbers, and making frequent and formidable demonstrations along the coast of South Carolina.

On the 30th of November, Major Gen. G. W. Smith, of the Georgia state forces, had, a few miles from Grahamville, administered to the enemy a most bloody and signal defeat, saving the road from threatened destruction, and securing the only feasible avenue of retreat for the garrison of Savannah, upon which city Gen. Sherman was rapidly closing, although it was even then regarded as uncertain what precise objective point on the coast he had in view.

Foiled in this effort to reach the Charleston and Savannah rail road, the Federals still hovered along the coast, endeavoring to effect permanent lodgments wherever there seemed a likelihood of achieving the object of their wishes. The few Confederate troops who could be spared for the protection of the road, were kept constantly on the alert, and moved from station to station as the danger of its threatened destruction grew imminent.

On the 15th of December the left section of the Battery — Lieut. Askew commanding — was ordered to Old Pocotaligo.[1] The contemplated attack upon the enemy on the Tullifinny having been abandoned, on the 18th this section was posted on the road leading to the landing on that river, where it remained until noon of the next day, when it was ordered to New Pocotaligo. Having occupied several positions in the vicinity of Old Pocotaligo during the ensuing few days, and the enemy failing to advance as was expected, the section was relieved from duty and directed to rejoin the Battery at Battery Means, which it did on the 23d. One section remained at Battery Means, and the other at Chisholmville until the last of the month, when the entire company was directed to return to its former camp on James island, which it reached on the morning of the 5th of January, 1865.

Two days afterwards the following special orders were issued from department head quarters:

HEAD QUARTERS, DEPARTMENT S. C., GEO. and FLA.
SPECIAL ORDERS, No. 6.

I. All men in excess of an effective total of sixty (60) men in the four-gun batteries of light artillery in this department, will be armed and drilled as infantry. They will be placed in special charge of an officer selected from the Battery, and will

---

[1] The Chatham Artillery, although most desirous of doing so, were not permitted the privilege of sharing in the immediate defense of the city of Savannah. In the judgment of the commanding general circumstances rendered it necessary that this Battery should remain where it was, on the line of the Charleston and Savannah rail road. Although not present upon the western lines, its services during the siege were important in keeping open the only available line of retreat for the garrison when the evacuation of the city became a military necessity.

habitually march with, and constitute a supporting force for their respective batteries. When the batteries of a battalion are united, the several infantry supports above provided for may be united, and will constitute a support for the battalion.

By command of

LIEUT. GEN. WM. J. HARDEE.

In pursuance of the foregoing order, and to carry the same into effect — having secured the requisite number of Enfield rifles — Captain Wheaton issued the following orders:

HEAD QUARTERS WHEATON'S LIGHT BATTERY,
Camp Colquitt, James Island, January 15, 1865.

In obedience to special order No. 6 from department head quarters, the following will constitute the order of detachments and infantry support in this Battery, viz:

Cannoneers.

1st Detachment.— Sergeant Gray; Corporals Crabtree, and Wylly; Privates Bowman, Charlton, Clark, Lyon, McDonald, Morse, and Theus.

2d Detachment.— Sergeant Garden; Corporals Baker, and O'Byrne; Privates Baynard, Cooke, Corbin, Hodges, Miller, McIntyre, and Washburn.

3d Detachment.— Sergeant Harden; Corporals Walker, and Morel; Privates Dunn, Hudson, Le Conte, Saussy, Stubbs, Silva, A. W., and Walker.

4th Detachment.— Sergeant Mitchell; Corporals Mallett, and Turner; Privates Champion, Farr, George, Joiner, M. Lampe, McCrary, Jones, F. P., and Thompson.

Drivers.

1st Detachment.— Privates Johnson, Lynch, McAvady, Tiernay, Manion, Jr., and Kenny.

2d Detachment.— Privates Broderick, Coleman, Leary, McVeigh, Malone, D., and Thompson.

3d Detachment.— Privates Haggerty, O'Brien, M., Slammon, Spence, Atkinson, and Myler.

4th Detachment.— Privates Hughes, Hayes, Kelly, Williamson, Lodkey, and Dreesen.

Litter Bearers.

Privates Veal, John Wilkes, Arera, and J. R. Farr.

Battery Wagon and Forge Drivers.

Privates J. E. Jones, Manion, Snr., Lamon, Golden, McIntyre, and Taggle.

Supernumeraries.

Privates W. J. Jones, Young, and O'Neil.

Cooks.

Privates P. O'Brien, Sumner, Morris, and McArthy.

Infantry Support.

Privates McNish, Baker, W. S. Clark, Dreese, Freeborn, Gilleland, Griffin, A. W. Hannon, Jacob Joiner, Joseph Joiner, Jaudon, Krenson, Kennickle, Lovel, Mongin, Minton, Wm. Miller, Makin, Patot, Perry, Remshart, John N. Silva, Sykes, J. J. Wilkes, and Williams.

Private T. W. McNish is hereby appointed drill sergeant of the infantry support, and will act as first sergeant of that force. He will be respected and obeyed accordingly.

Hereafter, in case of temporary absence or sickness of any regular driver, the driver whose horses are stabled opposite, will attend to the horses of the absent man.

In cases of emergency, or on the march, extra duty men and artificers will attend to teams, or drive, or perform any other duty that may be necessary.

By order of

JOHN F. WHEATON,
Captain Commanding.

CHAPTER IX.

The Chatham Artillery during the campaign in the Carolinas, and at the surrender of the Confederate forces under Gen. Joseph E. Johnston.

By the middle of January, Gen. Sherman had put his army in motion from Savannah for its march of plunder, house burning and desolation through the Carolinas.

Gen. Hood's army had well nigh suffered total annihilation in the recent Tennessee campaign; and its shattered, wounded remnants were slowly retiring to unite under Gen. Joseph E. Johnston in one last struggle for the Confederacy.

Gen. Lee, sore pressed in Virginia, could not spare a single man from the defense of the national capital. He needed tens of thousands more to enable him to cope, at least with the show of numerical equality, with the gathering hosts, which, as the locusts of Egypt, were swarming beneath the banners of Gen. Grant.

The fall of Fort Fisher, and the subsequent opening up by Gen. Scofield of facile communication between Wilmington and Goldsboro — the objective of Gen. Sherman — resulted from the inability of depleted Confederate garrisons to cope successfully with the overwhelming numbers concentrated against them.

Gen. Hardee,[1] with his eighteen thousand Confede-

---

[1] At a conference held on the 2d day of February, 1865, at Green's Cut station on the Augusta and Waynesboro rail road, in Burke

rate troops at detached points along the Carolina coast and elsewhere, composed in large measure of

---

county, Georgia, at which Gen. Beauregard, Lieut. Gen. Hardee, Maj. Gen. D. H. Hill and Maj. Gen. G. W. Smith were present, the following was the estimated strength of the forces in and about Augusta, and in the state of South Carolina, which it was thought could be relied on as effective to resist the advance of Gen. Sherman :

Gen. Hardee's Regular Infantry, P. A. C. S.,	8,000	
Militia and Reserves, . .	3,000	
	——	11,000
Light Artillery, . .	2,000	
Butler's Division, one-half only now available,	1,500	
	——	3,500

Total under command of Gen. Hardee in South Carolina, 14,500

Maj. Gen. Smith's Georgia Militia, . .	1,200	
Colonel Browne's Georgia Reserves, . .	250	
	——	1,450

Lieut. Gen. Lee's Corps, .	{ Only about ⅓ of	4,000
" " Cheatham's Corps,	which were reported	3,000
" " Stewart's Corps,	for active duty.	3,000
		—— 10,000

Artillery, Army of Tennessee, ...		800
Gen. Wheeler's Cavalry, ...		6,700

RECAPITULATION.

Total Infantry, ...	22,450
Light Artillery, ...	2,800
Cavalry, mounted and dismounted, . .	8,200

Grand Total, ...   33,450

Cheatham's and Stewart's corps had not arrived. The head of Cheatham's corps was expected to arrive in Augusta on the 4th or 5th inst., and the head of Stewart's on the 10th or 11th.

In view of Sherman's present position, his manifest advance towards Branchville from Pocotaligo and Coosawhatchie, the weakness of our forces, and the expected arrival of the reenforcements above referred to, it was deemed inadvisable to concentrate our forces at Branchville and there offer battle. During the pending negotiations for peace it was thought of the highest importance to hold Charleston and Augusta as long as it was humanly possible. Moreover, it being in violation of all maxims of the military art to adopt a place as a point of concentration which it was possible that the enemy with a largely superior force could reach before our columns could arrive, it was therefore concluded :

reserves and state forces recently brought into, and
unaccustomed to the hardships of actual service, and of

1st. That the line of the Combahee should be held as long as practicable, resisting the enemy strongly at all points.

2d. Should the enemy penetrate this line or turn it in force, Gen.
Hardee should retire with his forces — covering his rear with about
five hundred cavalry — towards Charleston, resisting the advance of
the enemy in that direction vigorously, behind every available creek,
river or swamp, whilst Wheeler, dividing his forces temporarily, should
fall back with the main portion in the direction of Columbia, checking the enemy's advance should he follow, and hold the line of the
Congaree until reenforcements could arrive ; the other portion of his
cavalry to fall back towards Augusta, covering that place.

3d. Should the enemy follow Hardee and indicate an attack on
Charleston, and whenever it should become evident that a longer
defense was impracticable, Gen. Hardee should abandon the place, and,
removing all valuable stores, hasten to form a junction with the forces
of Gen. Beauregard who would cover Columbia and take up the Congaree as a line of defense.

4th. That the infantry now on the line of Brier creek (about twenty-
five miles south of Augusta at the nearest point), should be removed
as soon as the stores were brought back, and take up a new position
along Spirit creek, about fifteen miles nearer, which should be fortified.
A four-gun battery with embrasures and heavy traverses was to be
placed on the Savannah river near the mouth of Spirit creek, and a
similar one at Sand-bar ferry ; both batteries to be aided by torpedoes
in the river.

5th. It was held in contemplation to send Lee's corps to Branchville,
and, in the event of the happening of the contingency alluded to in
the 2d and 3d resolutions, Maj. Gen. Stevenson commanding that corps
should retire towards the Congaree protected by the cavalry, where he
would watch and guard its crossings until the arrival of Generals
Beauregard and Hardee.

It was estimated by Gen. Hardee that 20,000 men at least would be
required for the proper defense of Charleston during the period of
twenty days, there being in that city an accumulation of supplies for
that space of time only.

The enemy moving with a certain number of days' rations for all
his troops, with the hope of soon establishing a base of supplies, in
reality had no lines of communication which could be cut or threatened ; his overwhelming force enabling him to pass into the interior
of the country like an ordinary movable column.

artillerists drawn from fixed batteries, who for the
first time were taking the field as infantry — was
incapable of offering effectual resistance to the advance
of the converging columns of Howard and Slocum,
each more than three times as large as any force he
could at any point concentrate in opposition. Full
four years of gigantic war under the most unfavorable
circumstances, and of ceaseless conflict with overwhelming odds, had well nigh consumed the manhood
and the substantial resources of the isolated and
bleeding Confederacy. Cut off from all communication with the outside world, with no resources save
such as were developed within her own confines,
pressed on all sides, with her lines of internal communication sadly deranged, with a depreciated currency, and an army poorly clad, badly fed, and without
pay, it was impossible longer to stem the torrent of
invasion with any good hope of ultimate success.
Sherman's march through the Carolinas was fore-
shadowed in his march through Georgia — in each
instance accomplished with ease, because there was
not in the country a Confederate force strong enough
to materially retard his progress. Charleston[1] fell
without a blow through the sheer force of circumstances, and that gallant city whose heroic resistance
had defied the fiercest assaults of an attacking enemy
through long years of danger and suffering — whose
advanced works, Sumter and Wagner, had given to
history memories of valor which will live with the
recollections of Leyden, and Malta, and Saragossa,
and Crema — abandoned of her defenders, was surren-

---

[1] As early as the 27th of December, 1864, Lieut. Gen. Hardee had
been directed by Gen. Beauregard commanding the military division
of the west, silently and cautiously to make all necessary preparations
for the evacuation of this city, and the withdrawal of the garrisons of

dered by her mayor to a lieutenant colonel of infantry,
commanding a negro regiment!

The knightly blade of the noble Hampton was

---

the various works erected for its defense, so soon as the contemplated
emergency should arise.

That order was subsequently repeated in the following terms:

CHARLESTON, S. C., December 31, 1864,

Lieut. Gen. W. J. Hardee commanding Dept. of
S. C., Geo., and Fla., Charleston, S. C.

General : I inclose herewith a copy of a telegram received to-day
from the President, relieving me at my request of the general command
of the departments of South Carolina, Georgia and Florida. My presence is absolutely required at this moment at Montgomery and with
the army of Tennessee, and I am unable to inform you when I will be
able to return in this direction. The interruption of rail road communication might render it impracticable to get back in time to be of
assistance to you should you require my aid suddenly. The telegram
of the President not being explicit as to the status of Augusta, I have
requested that it should be included in your department, as you now
have under you the whole of Wheeler's cavalry and nearly all the
available forces of Georgia, which are also required by you for the
defense of South Carolina. The defense of this city is so intimately
connected with that of the western portion of this state, that you will
consider it within the limits of your department until further orders
from the war department.

I have already given you all the verbal instructions possible for the
defense of Charleston and this state. The answer of the war department, not yet received, to my telegram of the 27th inst., will determine
whether, in the event of evacuating this city, you will retire towards
Georgia or North Carolina as a base. The first is your natural base,
but should you have reason to expect large reenforcements from the
latter state, you should, of course, retire in that direction.

You will apply to the defense of Charleston the same principle
applied to that of Savannah ; that is, defend it as long as compatible
with the safety of your forces. Having no reason at present to expect
succor from an army of relief, you must save your troops for the
defense of South Carolina and Georgia.

The fall of Charleston would necessarily be a terrible blow to the
Confederacy, but its fall with the loss of its brave garrison would be still
more fatal to our cause. You will, however, make all the preparations

powerless to save his beautiful home — the capital of his state — from the hand of the plunderer and the torch of the incendiary.

---

necessary for the possible evacuation of the city, and " clear your decks for action." Should it not take place, the trouble and expense of transportation will amount to little ; but should you be compelled to evacuate the city when unprepared, the loss of public property would be incalculable.

All the cotton in the city should be removed ; and if any be in the city at the time of its evacuation, it must be destroyed.

As already instructed, you should organize all your troops for the field, collecting sufficient transportation, ammunition and provisions for an active campaign. You must have depots of provisions and forage at several points in the interior of the state. Columbia would be a very suitable point — Florence also, if you expect to move in the direction of North Carolina. Augusta, Mayfield and Milledgeville must be depots for future operations.

Your defensive lines from the Savannah river would be as already explained to you.

1. The Combahee and Salkehatchie to Barnwell Court House, and thence to the Savannah river.

2. The Oshepoo and Salkehatchie to Barnwell Court House ; and thence to the Savannah river.

3. Edisto to Branchville, thence across towards Barnwell Court House.

4. Edisto and Caw-Caw Swamp or Rantowl's creek.

5. Edisto and Ashley.

Wheeler's cavalry must protect your front towards Savannah river, and your right flank from Barnwell Court House towards Augusta. At least the larger portion of his cavalry must be south of that river to watch the movements and check the progress of any force moving towards Augusta, or the interior of Georgia, until the rest of the cavalry and other forces could be sent to give battle to the enemy.

Please keep General Cobb and myself advised of your movements, and those of the enemy, that we may give you in time any assistance in our power. Hoping that you may be successful in holding Charleston and repelling any advance of the enemy, I remain,

Respectfully

Your Obedient Servant,

G. T. BEAUREGARD,

General.

The combined forces of Hampton, Wheeler and Butler could only skirmish heavily with the advancing Federal columns. They could not check them, and the battle of Bentonville clearly demonstrated alike the valor and the weakness of Gen. Johnston's army.

We may not now pause to follow in the footsteps of that invading army, or to chronicle the incidents of the campaign. Its desolating scars are still upon the land. The scenes of license, and plunder, and conflagration, and anguish, and death which it engendered, will not soon be forgotten. The damning record will live in all its deformity, known, read and abhorred of all men who have hearts to love the good, and contemn the evil.

The following is a diary of the movements of the Battery during the Carolina campaign :

On the 2d of February, 1865, the Chatham Artillery was ordered to Branchville, and reached that point on the 4th. The next day it proceeded by rail to Orangeburg. Two days afterwards it marched by dirt road for Columbia, with orders to report to Gen. Hampton ; and arriving there at ten o'clock A. M., on the 10th, encamped on the Congaree river in the vicinity of the city. The Battery was now assigned to duty with Butler's division of Hampton's cavalry.

On the 15th the Battery moved across the Congaree, and taking a position at Granby's, shelled the Federal camps all night. At day-dawn it retired to a hill about three hundred yards in rear of that position ; and, as the enemy commenced moving, opened fire upon their columns and continued this for two hours. Without an infantry support for the most of the time, and in this isolated position, the Chatham Artillery during this day contested the advance of the enemy, enduring a heavy fire from infantry and artillery.

Three men, viz: Corporal O'Byrne, and Privates Lovell and Tierney were wounded, and the Battery lost several horses killed and wounded.

To the resistance here encountered, and the severe shelling sustained at the hands of the Chatham Artillery at this point, Gen. Sherman alludes in his official report.

On the 17th the Battery received orders to move above Columbia, and occupying the bank of the river near the Saluda factory, to contest the crossing of the enemy. While on the march towards Columbia in the execution of this order, the fact was ascertained that the city was already in the possession of the advanced guards of the enemy, and, at the same time, Capt. Wheaton was notified that his Battery had been cut off, and that avoiding Columbia he must make his way, as rapidly and as best he could, and join Butler's division of cavalry at Kenyon's mills that night, if practicable.

After a forced march of about twenty-seven miles within sight and hearing of the enemy, and by unfrequented roads, the Battery succeeded in circumventing the city; and, eluding the pursuit of the Federals, reached Butler's division at Kenyon's mills at ten o'clock P. M., having lost ten men captured by the enemy during the day.

For several succeeding days the Battery skirmished with the enemy, checking the Federal advance as far as practicable.

February 20th. — Marched through Winnsboro, and halted for the night at Gladden's grove.

February 21st.— Retreated to Cloud's, and the next day, having forded the Catawba river at Land's ford, camped for the night on the opposite bank of the river. On the 23d the Battery was ordered to Charlotte, North Carolina, which village was reached on the morning of the 24th. There it remained in camp until the sixth of March. Information having been received of the evacuation of Fayetteville by the Confederate forces, the Chatham Artillery was directed to proceed to Smithfield. The recent rains had rendered the roads almost impassable. Men and animals floundered hour after hour in the mud and clay, and the wheels of the gun carriages sank down to their hubs. The Yadkin was so high that it could not be forded. A crazy flat was secured, however, and in this the Battery was safely transported piece-meal across. Upon the banks of this stream the company halted for twenty-four hours to shoe the battery animals, and make certain necessary repairs. The Haw was forded without accident, and Chapel hill reached on the 16th. Here, for the time being, the fatigues and the privations of the march were forgotten amid the hospitalities and attentions of the citizens of this pleasant village. The kind ladies, with their own fair hands, and sweet words of welcome and encouragement, generously dispensed the most abundant supplies. Every haversack was filled to overflowing with choicest viands, and the weary soldiers were sent on their way rejoicing, refreshed and invigorated. Amid the many depressing recollections of this gloomy campaign, the memory of the smiles, the cheering words, and the generosity of the ladies of Chapel hill lingers still in the grateful hearts of Chatham Artillerymen — a verdant oasis, redolent of richest perfumes, in the midst of a dreary waste.

Raleigh was reached on the 18th at noon. The Battery there rested during the 19th, and on the 21st, when within six miles of Smithfield, received orders to return to Raleigh. At this place the Battery remained until the 28th, when it proceeded in the direction of Hillsboro, and encamped in that vicinity on the 29th.

In obedience to orders from Gen. Beauregard the Chatham Artillery there reported to Col. Gonzales to be inspected and placed on the best possible footing for active service. Of thirty light batteries there concentrated — the most of them being unfit for field service — ten were to be chosen, and furnished at the expense of the others, with the best battery animals and equipments. Of these ten the Chatham Artillery was selected as one. It remained in the vicinity of Hillsboro until the sixth of April. It was a most difficult matter at this point to secure either rations for the men, or forage for the battery animals. The country for miles around was scoured for corn, and there was but one mill in the neighborhood where this could be ground. At times that mill could not run on account of the high water, and then the corn was issued to the men, who were compelled to shell and parch it in their camp fires as the only means of subsistence. Of meat, there was but little, and often none at all. From the quarter master and commissary departments no supplies could be procured.

Having received fifteen fresh horses, and having turned in the battery wagon, the company marched under orders to report to Gen. Joseph E. Johnston, then at Smithfield. Passing through Denham, Morrisville, Raleigh and Clayton, on the 10th of April the Battery reported at Smithfield, and was by Gen. Johnston assigned to duty with Loring's division of Stewart's Corps. It was subsequently placed in a battalion with Parker's Battery, under command of the senior captain. The Confederate army was then retiring in the direction of Greensboro, and the Battery retreated with Loring's division, crossing the Neuse and the Haw, and arriving at camp within five miles of Greensboro on the 16th. During the armistice the Battery remained at this point. On the retreat some ten battery animals had perished for lack of forage, and here great difficulty was experienced in procuring even a limited amount of corn, fodder and peas. The country was scoured for twenty-five miles round for forage.

A spirit of dissatisfaction prevailed in the army in anticipation of its early surrender; and numerous desertions occurred, accompanied by constant thefts of the transportation and artillery animals. A strong guard was posted for the protection of the battery animals belonging to the Chatham Artillery, and in honor of the vigilance and the patriotism of this company be it remembered that during these darkest days of impending ruin, of privations, and of horrid suspense, there occurred not a single desertion from its ranks, or the loss of a battery animal.

In anticipation of a renewal of hostilities the Confederate army was put in motion on the morning of the 26th, and while upon the march, some four miles from the village of Greensboro, the news of the surrender of the Confederate forces under Gen. Johnston was received. The column halted, and the Battery was parked.

The terms of capitulation specified in the first agreement of the 18th of April[1] had been disapproved at

---

[1] That agreement — in perfect accord with President Lincoln's policy at that time so far as it was known by, and had been communicated to his generals and the public generally — read as follows :

"Memorandum or basis of agreement made this 18th day of April A. D. 1865, near Durham's station in the state of North Carolina, by and between Gen. Joseph E. Johnston commanding the Confederate

Washington, and the following were mutually adopted by Generals Johnston and Sherman as a final basis of surrender:

---

army, and Maj. Gen. W. T. Sherman commanding the army of the United States, both present.

"I. The contending armies now in the field to maintain the *status quo* until notice is given by the commanding general of any one to his opponent, and reasonable time, say forty-eight hours, allowed.

"II. The Confederate armies now in existence to be disbanded, and conducted to their several state capitals, there to deposit their arms and public property in the state arsenal, and each officer and man to execute and file an agreement to cease from acts of war, and to abide the action of both State and Federal authorities. The number of arms and munitions of war to be reported to the chief of ordnance at Washington city, subject to the future action of the Congress of the United States, and in the meantime to be used solely to maintain peace and order within the borders of the states respectively.

"III. The recognition by the executive of the United States of the several state governments, on their officers and legislatures taking the oath prescribed by the constitution of the United States; and where conflicting state governments have resulted from the war, the legitimacy of all shall be submitted to the supreme court of the United States.

"IV. The reestablishment of all Federal courts in the several states, with powers as defined by the constitution and laws of congress.

"V. The people and inhabitants of all states to be guarantied, so far as the executive can, their political rights and franchise, as well as their rights of person and property, as defined by the constitution of the United States and of the states respectively.

"VI. The executive authority or government of the United States not to disturb any of the people by reason of the late war, so long as they live in peace and quiet, and abstain from acts of armed hostility, and obey the laws in existence at the place of their residence.

"VI. In general terms it is announced that the war is to cease; a general amnesty, so far as the executive of the United States can command, on condition of the disbandment of the Confederate armies, the distribution of arms, and the resumption of peaceful pursuits by officers and men hitherto composing said armies.

Not being fully empowered by our respective principals to fulfill these terms, we individually and officially pledge ourselves to promptly obtain authority, and will endeavor to carry out the above programme."

Terms of a military convention held this twenty-sixth (26th) day of April, 1865, at Bennett's house near Durham's station, N. C., between Gen. Joseph E. Johnston commanding the Confederate army, and Major Gen. W. T. Sherman commanding the United States army in North Carolina.

All acts of war on the part of the troops under Gen. Johnston's command to cease from this date.

All arms and public property to be deposited at Greensboro, to be delivered to an ordnance officer of the United States army.

Rolls of all the officers and men to be made in duplicate — one copy to be retained by the commander of the troops, and the other to be given to an officer to be designated by General Sherman.

Each officer and man to give his individual obligation in writing not to take up arms against the government of the United States until properly released from this obligation.

The side arms of officers, and their private horses and baggage to be retained by them.

This being done, all the officers and men will be permitted to return to their homes, not to be disturbed by the United States authority so long as they observe their obligation and the laws in force where they may reside.

W. T. SHERMAN,

Major Gen. commanding U. S. forces

in North Carolina.

J. E. JOHNSTON,

Gen. commanding C. S. forces

in North Carolina.

Approved.

U. S. Grant, Lieut. Gen.

Raleigh, North Carolina, April, 26, 1865.

The next day, the stipulations and fact of this surrender were communicated by the respective commanding generals to their armies, in the following orders :

HEAD QUARTERS, Army of Tennessee,
Near Greensboro, North Carolina, April 27, 1865.

GENERAL ORDERS, No. 18.

By the terms of a military convention made on the 26th inst. by Maj. Gen. W. T. Sherman U. S. army, and Gen. J. E. Johnston, C. S. army, the officers and men of this army are to bind themselves not to take up arms against the United States until properly relieved from this obligation, and shall receive guaranties from the United States officers against molestation by the United States authorities so long as they observe that obligation, and the laws in force where they reside.

For these objects, duplicate muster rolls will be made immediately, and, after the distribution of the necessary papers, the troops will march under their officers to their respective states and there be disbanded, all retaining personal property.

The object of this convention is pacification to the extent of the commanders who made it.

Events in Virginia which broke every hope of success by war, imposed on its generals the duty of sparing the blood of this gallant army, and saving our country from further devastation, and our people from ruin.

J. E. JOHNSTON,
General.

HEAD QUARTERS, Military Division of the Mississippi.
In the Field, *Raleigh, N. C.*, April 27, 1865.

SPECIAL FIELD ORDERS, No. 65.

The general commanding announces a further suspension of hostilities, and a final agreement with Gen. J. E. Johnston, which terminates the war as to the armies under his command, and the country east of the Chattahoochee.

Copies of the terms of convention will be furnished Maj. Generals Schofield, Gillmore and Wilson, who are specially charged with the execution of the details in the department of

North Carolina, the department of the south, and at Macon, and in Western Georgia.

Capt. Jasper Myers, Ord. Officer U. S. A., is hereby designated to receive the arms, etc., at Greensboro, and any commanding officer of a post may receive the arms of a detachment, and see that they are properly stored and accounted for.

General Schofield will procure at once the necessary blanks and supply the other army commanders, that uniformity may prevail; and great care must be taken that all the stipulations on our part be fulfilled with the most scrupulous fidelity, whilst those imposed on our hitherto enemies be received in a spirit becoming a brave and generous army.

Army commanders may at once loan to the inhabitants such of the captured mules and horses, wagons and vehicles as can be spared, to relieve present wants and encourage the inhabitants to renew their peaceful pursuits, and to restore the relations of friendship among our fellow citizens and countrymen.

Foraging will forthwith cease, and when necessity or long marches compel the taking of forage, or provisions, or any kind of private property, compensation will be made on the spot; or, when the disbursing officers are not provided with funds, vouchers will be given in proper form payable at the nearest military depot.

By command of
MAJ. GEN. W. T. SHERMAN.

On the 1st of May, 1865 — its seventy-ninth anniversary — the company was paroled. Its guns, and horses and equipments were turned in on the 2d. The guns were parked at Greensboro with the rest of the Confederate light artillery, and were not formally received by any Federal officer. The Battery surrendered consisted of four twelve-pounder Napoleon guns. Two of them had been manufactured at the Confederate arsenal at Macon, Georgia, and the other two were Federal guns which had been captured at the battle of Olustee and turned over to the company by the general commanding in token of his appreciation of the distinguished services and gallant conduct of the Battery during that memorable engagement. It was with feelings of peculiar regret that the company parted with these guns which their valor had won. At the time of the surrender, there were with the Battery about one hundred men present for duty. The battery animals were generally unfit for service, having suffered severely during late marches from fatigue and lack of forage. The sergeants were all dismounted, and some of the caissons were drawn by only four horses.

The troops were not paid off, but the men received each, *one dollar in silver*, in payment of no specified services and for no designated period, but receipted for upon rolls specially prepared and intended simply as vouchers for the quarter masters.

The following final order of General Johnston was received with profound emotion by the army; and the farewell words of this great chieftain sank like lead into the hearts of brave men, who saw in the surrender of Generals Lee and Johnston the downfall of that beloved Confederacy for whose existence they had so long and so sternly struggled in tears, and agony, and privations and blood :

HEAD QUARTERS, Army of Tennessee,
Near Greensboro, N. C., May, 2, 1865.

GENERAL ORDERS, No. 22.

Comrades: In terminating our official relations, I earnestly exhort you to observe faithfully the terms of pacification agreed upon, and to discharge the obligations of good and peaceful citizens at your homes, as well as you have performed the duties of thorough soldiers in the field. By such a course you will best secure the comfort of your families and kindred, and restore tranquillity to our country.

You will return to your homes with the admiration of our people, won by the courage and noble devotion you have displayed in this long war.

I shall always remember with pride the loyal support and generous confidence you have given me. I now part with you with deep regret, and bid you farewell with feelings of cordial friendship, and with earnest wishes that you may hereafter have all the prosperity and happiness to be found in the world.

J. E. JOHNSTON,
General.

The following is the form of the parole given:

GREENSBORO, North Carolina, May 1st, 1865.

In accordance with the terms of the military convention entered into on the 26th day of April, 1865, between Gen. Joseph E. Johnston commanding the Confederate army, and Major Gen. W. T. Sherman commanding the United States army in North Carolina, ... of Wheaton's Light Battery has given his solemn obligation not to take up arms against the government of the United States until properly released from this obligation; and is permitted to return to his home, not to be disturbed by the United States authorities so long as he observes this obligation, and obeys the laws in force where he may reside.

JOHN F. WHEATON,
Captain C. S. A., Commanding Battery.

Hobart Ford,
Captain and A D C., U. S. A., Special Commissioner.

On the 3d of May, 1865, having discharged the last sad duties devolved upon it by virtue of the terms of the surrender, the members of the Chatham

Artillery with heavy hearts entered upon their home-ward march, in company with Loring's division and the men of Parker's Light Battery. After crossing the Yadkin these two artillery companies parted com-pany with the infantry, and continued the march together until the 8th, when they separated — the Chatham Artillery taking the direct road for Augusta. The Catawba river was crossed on a pontoon bridge. Marched through Chesterville, crossed the Broad river in a flat, passed through Newberry, crossed the Saluda river in a flat, and reached Hamburg opposite Augusta on the 14th. There the men rested during the 15th, and on the 16th of May, 1865, were formally disbanded to their respective homes in compliance with the specific orders of Gen. Johnston and the express terms of the surrender. During the entire march — while in other commands straggling and disorganization obtained to a fearful extent — the organization of the Chatham Artillery was carefully preserved. Guard duty was regularly performed to the last moment, and good order maintained. None left the company except such as were too weak to endure the fatigues of the march. These were placed upon the cars at Greensboro and at Salisbury. On the morning that the company was finally disbanded, ninety men answered to their names at roll call. Of the thousands returning from Greensboro — so far as it can be stated with certainty — the Chatham Artil-lery was the only military organization which reached the city of Augusta intact. Day by day on the home-ward march, companies and whole regiments melted away. Thus, to the latest moment of its military existence, did this company maintain inviolate that obedience to, and love of order, which always charac-terized it in such a remarkable degree. During this homeward march the company had transportation for baggage and rations, and at Augusta transportation home by rail road and steam boat was furnished the men, as far as practicable, by the Federal quarter masters.

CHAPTER X.

Concluding observations.

Thus ended the connection of the Chatham Artillery with the military service of the Confederate states. Commencing on the 3d of January, 1861, with the occupation of Fort Pulaski under orders from the governor of Georgia, it continued until the last gun of the war had been fired, until, by the surrender of the Confederate forces under Generals Lee and Johnston, the last hope of achieving the independence of the southern Confederacy had been extinguished in the gloom of despair.

Although the military history of this Battery is less bloody, and in the record of its services may be enumerated fewer scenes of carnage, imminent dangers and hair breadth escapes than occur in the history of many other organizations in the Confederate army, of the members of no company can it be more truthfully said, they did their whole duty cheerfully, intelligently, efficiently and patriotically at all times and under all circumstances. The appreciation of this fact, even amid these dark days of disappointment and of poverty, is a source of pride and of honor priceless in the consolations which it brings.

Although the rich goal of national independence was not attained, the happy consciousness remains of self-respect preserved, of honor vindicated, of manhood declared, and of every honest effort expended in the brave defense of principle and property. Overcome,

but not conquered — defeated, but not humiliated —
impoverished, but not degraded — oppressed, and yet
proud in spirit — such to-day is the condition of the
south. Federal armies — attracting to themselves under the stimulus of extraordinary exertions, and by
virtue of most prodigal bounties, multitudes of recruits
from the new and mercenaries from the old world — in
obedience to the commands of a military dictator, and
at the expense of blood, and treasure, and right, com-
passed a physical solution of the question of comparative strength in favor of superior numbers and greater
resources. They did not determine the validity or
impropriety of the moral propositions involved in this
gigantic struggle. The sword never does, it never
has, and it never can submit any other than a physical
arbitrament in matters of conscience, of abstract
principle and of inalienable right. The dismember-
ment of Poland was accomplished by warlike measures
which commended themselves to the entire approbation of the arbitrary, grasping monarchs by whom
they were inaugurated and sustained ; and yet the life
blood of that nation has ever been held sacred, and
its death agonies perpetuated in honor, in story and in
song, and the action of the invading armies which
blotted out from the sisterhood of nations a brave
people struggling for liberty and national existence,
condemned by every lover of freedom, by the voice of
civilization, and the verdict of impartial history. To-
day the causes which brought about the Confederate
revolution are morally as unaffected by the issues of
the contest as they were at the moment of its inception. The Roman motto, *exitus acta probat*, is as falla-
cious as it is antiquated. The subsequent acts of
radical rule justify each day more and more emphatically the necessity which was laid upon the south to

maintain her honor, and manhood and self-respect,
even at the expense of wounds, and desolations and
death. Clouds of fanaticism cannot forever darken
the sunlight of truth and justice. The error of the
present will be corrected by the calm verdict of the
future, and the day will come when the moral record
of the struggle of the Confederate states for life, and
right, and liberty and property shall stand forth jus-
tified, and honored, and admired in the hearts of all
men who possess the knowledge to discern, the honesty
to appreciate, and the candor to confess.[1]   " However
sore her calamities, all is not yet lost to our bleeding
and beloved South. She still retains that which to
every true man is infinitely dearer than property or

---

[1] Any doubts heretofore existing or expressed with reference to the
right of, and the obligations resting upon the southern states, just
when they did, to make one bold, decided, manly, vigorous effort in
behalf of liberty and right, and honor and property, have been entirely
removed from the mind of every candid observer by the recent acts
of Federal legislation, the expressed policy of the United States, and
the avowed wishes and purposes of the masses of the North. The
necessity for, and the justice of the Confederate struggle for independence find amplest vindication in the conduct and aims, and dealings
of those who were and are most violent in the denunciation of its
inspiration and its ends.

In all wars guided by chivalric principles, said the knight of Brit-
tany, true soldiers never injure the "tillers of the ground."

The stern Du Guesclin when on his deathbed, desired his old companions in arms to remember that "neither the clergy, nor women,
nor children, nor poor people were their enemies," and the charge
came with peculiar propriety from him, for his past life could furnish
no instance of needless severity.

After the splendid victory of Poictiers, the young Edward in the
midst of that elevation produced by as extraordinary and unexpected
success as had ever crowned the arms of any commander, came forth
to meet the captive king with all the marks of regard and sympathy
that could be suggested by the most high toned magnanimity,
administered comfort to him amidst his misfortunes, paid the tribute

life. She retains her moral wealth — the glory of
her Jacksons, her Johnsons, her Lees and her Davises,
and of all who have nobly died or suffered in her
cause. These are her imperishable jewels ; and since
little else is left to her, these shall be cherished with
the greater love, with the more enthusiastic and
undying devotion.''

From its most northern limit to its southern verge,
from the western hills to its sea washed eastern shore,
the consecrated soil of the Confederacy has been

---

of praise due to his valor, ordered a repast to be prepared in his tent
for the royal prisoner, and himself served at the captive's table as if
he had been one of his retinue. To John in captivity were extended
the honors of a king. While riding through London to the Savoy,
the French captive monarch was mounted on a white and superbly
equipped war horse, while the prince, his conqueror, rode by his side
on a little black palfrey — a further illustration of that kind consideration which one true knight always showed to his brother in arms.

The lessons of a high toned past find but small observance at the
hands of this retrograded present. Magnanimity to a brave, unfortunate, and overcome people, who have in good faith accepted the issue
of the struggle, however distasteful and ruinous, seems to be utterly
ignored. Those high born impulses of true generosity and manhood
which should characterize the conqueror, are neither remembered nor
observed. A liberal and dignified consideration for the feelings, necessities and welfare of the vanquished and impoverished, apparently
belongs to a contemned period of Roman virtue, the dead chivalry
of a heroic age, now numbered with a neglected past, and the despised
teachings of the New Testament dispensation. *Væ victis* is the one
malignant cry of the conqueror, whose every act but adds fresh
indignities and injuries to the fanaticism and oppressions of the past.

For the outpouring of these vials of wrath, accepted theories are
overturned, lawless passions invoked, pledges violated, wholesome
regulations discarded, and government itself despoiled of its legitimate functions.

Even funeral honors to a noble Confederate, whose record like that
of Bayard and Sidney is without reproach, are publicly and ruthlessly
forbidden. Petty hate usurps the province of common humanity and
customary courtesy. Strange that malignity, which, not content with
oppressing the living and attempting the degradation of the unfortu-

baptized by the reddest blood of the noblest of the land. Along the hill sides, by the swiftly rolling rivers, in the silent valleys and within the dark shadows of our woods, they lie — the brave, the honored dead. Hallowed by this crimson tide, precious for all time must be the memories of these ensanguined fields.

On the entablature of an ancient gate-way leading towards a resting place for the dead, is an inscription in which the soul is sublimely celebrated as *superstes*

---

nate, denies the tears of sorrow and the homage of devotion at the grave of the pure patriot, the true hero.

> " They err who count it glorious to subdue
> By conquest far and wide, to overrun
> Large countries, and in field great battles win,
> Great cities by assault ; what do these worthies
> But rob and spoil, burn, slaughter and enslave
> Peaceable nations neighboring or remote,
> Made captive, *yet deserving freedom more*
> *Than those their conquerors*, who leave behind
> Nothing but ruins, wheresoe'er they rove,
> And all the flourishing works of peace destroy ;
> Then swell in pride, and must be titled gods,
> Till conqueror Death *discovers them scarce men*,
> Rolling in brutish vices and deformed,
> Violent or shameful death their due reward."

It were well for these fanatical leaders to pause for one moment, in the midst of their unbridled career of oppression and lawless legislation, and ponder these words of warning and of truth which Lord Macaulay puts in the mouth of Milton : " When will rulers learn that where liberty is not, security and order can never be. We talk of absolute power, but all power hath limits, which, if not fixed by the moderation of the governors, will be fixed by the force of the governed. Sovereigns may send their opposers to dungeons ; they may clear out a senate house with soldiers ; they may enlist armies of spies ; they may hang scores of the disaffected in chains at every cross road ; but what power shall stand in that frightful time when rebellion hath become a less evil than endurance ? Who shall dissolve that terrible tribunal, which, in the hearts of the oppressed, denounces against the oppressor the doom of its wild justice ? Who shall repeal the law of self defense ? What arms or discipline shall resist the strength of famine and despair ? "

corpori caduco — surviving the frail body. The inscription is old — its letters are fast fading from the stone, but it transfers itself to the mind of every beholder with all the freshness and vigor which characterized it when first traced by the graver's chisel centuries ago. Those occasional head boards — with their brief inscriptions fast yielding to the obliterating influences of time — placed by the kind hands of surviving comrades to mark the spot where fell the brave in arms, will soon perish under the disintegrating action of the winds and storms of the changing seasons. Even the general mound which covers the accumulated dead of the battle field will lose its outlines, but the noble spirit which animated that sleeping dust, the soul of patriotism which led them to give to their country their loves and their lives, will ever remain *superstes corpori caduco*. In those voiceless songs which in quiet hours we sing in our own thoughts, this mental refrain will remind ever of present and future honor for this immortal dust, of hope for the oppressed nation whose sons evinced such devotion to her cause.

The waves of the ocean as they break along our shore will sing an anthem of praise in honor of the illustrious dead. The everlasting hills will remain the living witnesses of their triumphs. The silent valleys will become vocal with their historic memories, and every river, and flood, and mountain, and plain will proclaim their deeds of valor. Long will the verdant grass perpetuate, and the over-arching trees cover with their protecting shadows those ramparts which their labor constructed, and their courage defended. Fair hands will, each year, with vernal flowers fresh, and spotless, and redolent of sweetest perfumes, garland the graves of the Confederate dead. Young and old will venerate the heroic memories of the Confederate struggle for independence, and children's children learn with their earliest breath to lisp the names of the great chieftains of the south, and with their youngest emotions, to admire and emulate their illustrious examples. Responsively will each heart beat to the passing wind as in low murmurs it breathes ever a requiem for these departed heroes; while the listening ear will obedient catch the warning voice of the Muse of history keeping her vestal vigils near each grass grown mound, as she repeats to the pilgrim at these national shrines of liberty, of honor, of patriotism, and of pure devotion, *siste viator, herorem calcas.*

Although

>   *   *   "Sepulchral columns wrestle but in vain
> With all subduing time ; her cankering hand
> With calm deliberate malice wasted them ;
> Worn on the edge of days the brass consumes,
> The busto moulders, and the deep cut marble
> Unsteady to the steel gives up its charge,"

nothing can impair the fair and enduring proportions of that monument which the gratitude of a good and patriotic people should erect in the heart of the south to the memory of the illustrious dead of the Confederate revolution — a monument unseen by mortal eye, yet far more imposing than the mausoleum of the Egyptian king — lifting its pure summit far above the region of commingled lights and shadows, and resting ever in that eternal sunlight where the clouds of envy, the vapors of detraction, and the shadows of fanaticism never rise — a monument more beautiful and bright than Parian marble — more lasting than brass, and more vocal in the undying memories which cluster about it than the fabled statue of Memnon.

The moral wealth of high resolves, fearless purposes, noble exertions and generous sacrifices in the
cause of truth, justice, liberty, property and honor —
the appreciation of duty performed and manhood
vindicated — the consolations which flow from a consciousness of rectitude in the high endeavor, the
record of brave deeds, the memories of a heroic past,
and the rich legacy of the valor and the devotion of
fathers, and brothers, and sons, are all that remain to
cheer the hearts of those who knew best, and loved,
and upheld the once puissant Confederacy in the days
of her grand armies and eventful struggles.

All else seems lost, and as memory dwells upon
the proud hopes which have been extinguished in the
gloom of despair, as we reckon the grievous disap-
pointments and losses which have fallen upon the
land, as we experience the miseries of the present,
and mark no cheering bow of promise amid the dark
clouds which hang upon the brow of the future, as
we embalm in the sacred recesses of our own bosoms
the recollections of a hallowed struggle, and in sorrow
recognize the fact that the eye will never more
brighten at sight of the loved emblem of a young
nation battling for its primal existence, full high
advanced in the pure light of heaven, and appreciate
the reasons why these things are so, with what peculiar pathos do the following mournful strains sink into
the heart!

> " Furl that Banner! for 'tis weary;
>   Round its staff 'tis drooping dreary;
>   Furl it, fold it, it is best,
>   For there's not a man to wave it,
>   And there's not one left to lave it
>   In the blood which heroes gave it;

And its foes now scorn and brave it :
  Furl it, hide it, let it rest.

Take that Banner down ! 'tis tattered,
Broken is its staff and shattered,
And the valiant hosts are scattered
  O'er whom it floated high.
Oh ! 'tis hard for us to fold it ;
Hard to think there's none to hold it ;
Hard that those who once unrolled it
  Now must furl it with a sigh.

Furl that Banner ! furl it sadly ;
Once ten thousands hailed it gladly,
And ten thousands wildly, madly
  Swore it would forever wave.
Swore that foemen's sword could never
Hearts like their's entwined dissever,
'Till that flag should float forever
  O'er their freedom or their grave.

Furl it ! for the hands that grasped it,
And the hearts that fondly clasped it
  Cold and dead are lying low ;
And that Banner, it is trailing,
While around it sounds the wailing
  Of its people in their woe ;
For though conquered, they adore it ;
Love the cold dead hands that bore it ;
Weep for those who fell before it !
*   *   *   *   *
And oh ! wildly they deplore it
  Now to furl and fold it so.
    30

Furl that Banner! true 'tis gory ;
Yet 'tis wreathed around with glory,
And 'twill live in song and story,
　　Though its folds are in the dust ;
For its fame on brightest pages
Penned by poets and by sages
Shall go sounding down through ages ;
　　Furl its folds though now we must.

Furl that Banner ! softly, slowly !
Treat it gently, it is holy,
　　For it droops above the dead.
Touch it not — unfold it never,
Let it droop there furled forever,
　　For its people's hopes are dead.

INDEX.

Printed in Dunstable, United Kingdom